O BOXES

OUR LIFE IN BOXES

RICHARD IRWIN

TATE PUBLISHING
AND ENTERPRISES, LLC

Our Life in Boxes

Published by Tate Publishing & Enterprises, LLC
127 E. Trade Center Terrace | Mustang, Oklahoma 73064 USA
1.888.361.9473 | www.tatepublishing.com

Tate Publishing is committed to excellence in the publishing industry. The company reflects the philosophy established by the founders, based on Psalm 68:11,
"The Lord gave the word and great was the company of those who published it."

Cover design by Albert Ceasar Compay
Interior design by Mary Jean Archival

Published in the United States of America

ISBN: 978-1-68301-988-6
Biography & Autobiography / Personal Memoirs
16.03.03

INTRODUCTION

My working life began the day I joined the navy. I was nineteen. That was the first day I was on my own away from family and friends. From that day forward, I was never in one place more than a few years, always going to something and somewhere new. In the navy, I went from a diesel submarine to a nuclear submarine after getting training for each. My training included submarine operational systems, electronics, nuclear physics, and special training in nuclear power plant operation. For a landlubber born in Montana, spending time submerged a few hundred feet below the ocean waves at various times over a six-year period was not what I had imagined would be my vocation in life. But then again, getting an A in beer drinking in college sort of set the stage as I was given a choice of going on academic probation or doing something else—like joining the navy. My trek to Baghdad, Iraq, started from there.

Between the navy and Baghdad came places like San Diego, California, where I worked as an electronic technician for a small company that supplied the commercial fishing industry with positioning devices. It also made thermal sensors for the Apollo space program. From there, I worked in the quality control department for another company. But then, after a few years, I moved my family back to upstate New York, close to my wife's parents. I had married my wife, Jean, there in 1960. I got a job as an X-ray technician for large metal castings to look for defects. A little while later, I moved into mainframe computer field maintenance. The urge to return to college raised its head, so I applied and got accepted under a general studies program at the New York University in Albany. I graduated with a BS in business management. (I started, at nineteen, as a chemical engineering student before the navy and then changed to a political science major after the navy.)

With my degree in hand, I changed jobs and became a contract administrator for a company that specialized in overhauling some navy training reactors. My previous training in nuclear power gave me the edge I needed. And so began a different level of job movements that took me back, first, to the state I left to join the navy. I continued as a contract administrator involved in the building of twin nuclear power plants at the Hanford Nuclear Reservation in Washington. However, after about five years, the antinuclear advocates had managed to shut down most of the nuclear plant construction around the country, causing the state agency I was with to begin downsizing. I volunteered to be one of the people to go.

Seeing the handwriting on the wall, I had already begun to see what else was out there. That led me to work offshore in places like Saudi Arabia, Turkey, Denmark, Bosnia, Russia, and Iraq. In between these places were in-country jobs in Texas, North Carolina, California, and Indiana.

Finally, throughout those thirty-eight years of movement in life, I must recognize the impact I had on my family. They had to adjust their own lives to my job and location changes. And they did it well. Jean and I have five very successful children and eleven grandchildren who are destined for their own successes. Our great-grandchildren will continue the story of successes. I was told by a couple of Russians, and later by a couple of Bosnians, after telling them about my family that I was a very rich person. I truly believe that.

A reflection on how a person growing up in America can view the world and America's place in it:

"I think I'll write a book," I said.

"What are you going to write about?" I replied.

"Well," I fired back, "I've done a few things in my life that might be interesting to some people."

"Oh?" I queried skeptically. "Name something you did; give me an example."

"Okay, try this out."

Jean and I were on a tour, back in 1991, to the underground cities in Cappadocia located in central Turkey. The tour bus having stopped for fuel, and us for lunch, gave us some extra time to look around the small village where we had stopped. We had gone into a small souk, and I was sifting through a soup-bowl-sized wicker basket holding a bunch of loose coins that sat on a cluttered counter. The clutter consisted of various countertop things that are found in a small store in the middle of an old Turkish town catering to bus tours carrying tourists like Jean and me from various parts of the world. There were coins in the basket from some of these same countries lying next to or on top of each other. As I sifted, an American nickel came to the surface of the pile. It looked in fair shape, so I examined it further, turning it over in my hand. It was a 1938 Buffalo nickel, the year of my birth! Obviously, I had to have it. Ten thousand Turkish lira put the nickel my pocket. That was about three US dollars back then.

I thought it was fascinating that I would find such a coin in the middle of Turkey. But then again, the history of Turkey is vast and goes back a long way. Sorting through the coins was indeed a history lesson itself. I remember coins from England, Germany, Holland, and coins of other countries I no longer have in my recallable memory.

Jean and I were taking the tour to Cappadocia because of a brochure we picked up in the vestibule of St. Mary's Catholic Church in Izmir. I had been working in Turkey as a finance manager on a road project for an American company. We found that, among other attractions, the brochure showed an underground church carved out of the soft rock—probably sandstone—hills, carved with the appropriate ceiling support columns just like you would see in a Greek Orthodox church up on top of the ground anywhere in Byzantine. Obviously, the chiseled-out area didn't need the columns, but apparently, the church did to round out its appropriate architecture. That made us curious about what else might be down below. Why would people, in this case, Christians, want to live underground? Well, you would have to study first-century Roman history when Christianity was becoming active in this Roman-controlled area of Turkey and then later when the Arabs took control around the eleventh century to get the answer.

"That's your example?" I laughingly sneered. "Don't write a book. Stick with reading someone else's book."

"Come on, now!" I countered. "Okay, here's a better example. I'll even use another coin as a prop."

I wasn't prepared for the challenge to my example. So I went to a storage box of coins I kept in the attic for my rebuttal to the challenge. Actually, the box is a wooden wine-shipping box that Jean and I used when we brought some bottles of Italian wine home from a visit there one year. It had various types and amounts of coins and paper money inside, which had accumulated from what was in our pockets and had been thrown into the box each time we returned from some place or each time I came home from one of my jobs overseas.

I began to sort through the box just as I had done to the basket in the Suk in Turkey. Then it occurred to me. The money in my storage box was much more of a mix of countries than what I had found in the Turkish wicker basket! That meant that the history existing in my storage box would be more pervasive and interesting, if only to me, because, to paraphrase Walter Cronkite in his *You Are There* TV series, "I was there." In addition to the coinage, I had thrown paper money in as well. I found after sorting the bills I had money from twenty-two different countries. Well, I now need to sort out this history according to the coins and paper in my box and not the basket in the Suk. My rebuttal will have to wait because my "other coin" is really many coins now.

During this coin search, I noticed a few other boxes lying around other closets and places in the house. Some coins made it into these boxes too, but the real purpose of these other boxes was to store all the non-money stuff I had taken out of my other pockets or collected over the years. It turns out that I have the history of my working life spread around the house in a bunch of little boxes. To top it off, as I walked from room to room searching for the boxes, I passed by paintings hanging on the walls that Jean and I had collected during our travels, not to mention the figurines on display tables.

"Look," I said, "this story is taking on a broader character than I anticipated. What I need to do is sort out all the stuff in all my boxes to see what kind of life I lead as told from these bits of paper, identification tags, art work, plaques, and other things as well as the coins I stored in the first box. I've even stored some of my life on our walls that hold the paintings we brought from each country or the objects of art placed on stands. The coin I said I'd use as a prop will have to fit into the larger picture now."

"Okay, sounds interesting," I mused.

1

Before I get into the boxes, let me set my stage. Jean and I have the household-moving technique down pat. Even before we were married, as individuals, we moved around a bit, although I can claim more moves than she can. Jean's first move was out of Porter Corners, New York, when she was eighteen. Initially, she traveled to work from home. She had gotten a job in Saratoga Springs about ten miles south on Route 9N. After a few months, she changed jobs, which eventually took her to New York City. The Saratoga company had been bought out, and the new owners moved the work down there. That was her first move. But she found that the city was no place for a country girl like her. She finally ended up at a job in Albany commuting from Saratoga. She eventually moved a couple times around Saratoga.

For me, after getting an A in beer drinking at the local Jesuit College in Spokane, Washington, I decided joining the navy was better than academic probation. My brother,

Clark, was attending the same university at the time. He was a senior. He's the one who gave me the heads-up as to what coming. I found out later that he was contemplating joining the Jesuits, so it made sense that he would be given the task of informing his brother to shape up. I couldn't get away from school, though, as the navy sent me to schools in various places and then sent me to see the world. Actually, the navy sent me to sea on a submarine. From the navy's perspective, seeing the world was secondary. But for me, it was primary. The first time I saw the ocean was as a child from Montana, on a visit to one of my uncles in Portland, Oregon. All I saw then were big waves. The next time I saw the ocean was when I joined the navy. So for me, it was primary. At the same time, choosing submarine duty just came out of the blue. When I met with the recruiter, his questioning led him straight to offering me the chance to get into the nuclear power program. There weren't many nukes at sea at that time, but a lot were being planned and built. They needed crew. As it turned out, my education and general character apparently fit the mold. I remember saying to myself as I left the office after signing on, "What is this nuclear power stuff?" I hadn't reached that level of science yet. But what the heck, it sounded interesting.

I began to dwell on what I had just got myself into. It was intriguing. It was a world I had never imagined or considered. I was still a naive student who was about to enter the real world. I began to wonder what it would be like on a submarine. And what was the difference between the submarine I saw in movies and one that was nuclear powered? It didn't take long after boot camp to find out. During my first years in the navy, I learned a fundamental difference between WWII submarines and those of the future. I was first assigned to a diesel-powered boat before going on board a nuclear-powered one. (As an aside, we submariners were proud to call our submarines boats even though their size qualified them to be called ships. The story goes that some admiral in the navy's past did not have much good to say about this new class of warships being brought into the navy's armada. To give them the recognition of being a ship was beyond his tolerance, thus he always referred to them as boats. To his consternation, I'm sure, being called a boat gave us submariners a special status.)

Here's a small comparison of the old versus the new in submarine capability. As a matter of practice, nuclear submarines heading out to sea submerge as soon as the harbor buoy is passed and surface just before the buoy when coming back to port. (As another aside, most of my navy time after school was spent underwater.)

A diesel submarine can be described as a surface craft that can submerge under the water, but only for a short time. And that time is relatively short, around fourteen hours. The time could be extended if the boat had a snorkel system that allowed the diesel engines to be run while submerged. Use of air-pollutant-absorbing substances also could extend the time.

USS *Bream* SSK243

The snorkel system could only be used at periscope depth, however, and only in fairly calm waters. The snorkel is an extendable tube, like a periscope, tied to the ventilation system that provided the air needed for the engines as well as the crew. This tube would be extended to just above the surface to allow a suction to be taken on the atmosphere to supply the needed air to the engines. At the same time, some of the air coming in could be diverted to ventilate the boat. We could proceed on the snorkel for as long as sea conditions or mission orders allowed. If the sea became choppy—a condition that occurred quite often—it became difficult to maintain depth, causing the boat to change a few feet up or down. The wave action on the surface was hard to work against. To protect from water entering the snorkel tube and into the diesel engines, sensors at the top controlled the position of the valve at the top of the tube to be shut or opened as needed. Unfortunately for the crew, a shut valve meant the diesels would take suction on the inside of the boat, creating a vacuum until it opened again. During the process, your body felt like it went immediately to ten thousand feet and your ears took a while making the adjustment.

The normal undersea operating conditions, of course, were based on power provided by large batteries installed in the lowest portion of the boat's inner hull. Electric motor drive would take the propulsion power from the batteries and not the diesel engines'. Without the snorkel bringing in fresh air, the crew was dependent on the quality of air at the time of diving. Fourteen hours without refreshing the atmosphere was about the limit of available oxygen, and the increased amount of carbon dioxide would become a problem for the crew. This was not a problem in the normal operation of the boat. It was just a condition to be aware of and to be dealt with. Anyway, we did have options to extend the time below, but we did not use them unless operational conditions warranted.

There was one time though, I recall, where we did use the extra measures to allow us to remain submerged beyond the limit. We were doing some surveillance of some ships and other items of interest in a hostile area of the Sea of Japan. During our patrol, one of our antennas shorted out as a result of a leaking water seal. Seawater conducts electricity extremely well. The antenna was important to our data gathering. We had to surface to make repairs. The captain had observed through the periscope there was a fog bank in the area that we could use to maintain our cover. I and our chief in charge of the electronic gear went topside to replace the antenna. Unfortunately, it was not repairable at sea. During the time on the surface, our operating detection equipment alerted the captain that ships we didn't want to expose ourselves to were in the area. And as it turned out, we weren't successful in remaining undetected, so we dove quickly and prepared for silent running. For the next three days, we took evasive actions submerged as we moved steadily out of the area. That obviously took us well beyond the fourteen hours. But our boat had oxygen bottles installed in the ballast tanks, which allowed us to maintain our oxygen level for a time. It was more difficult to deal with the CO_2. If you don't get rid of the CO_2, any amount of oxygen will not be sufficient to support life. We had this white powdery chemical absorbent we spread out on a large surface, such as the top of a bunk cover or some other flat surface. We spread it out in each compartment. The medic kept a monitoring effort going so that we would know where we stood. At the end of the third day, we were about out of oxygen from the tanks, and the CO_2 absorbent was reaching its capacity with no more to spread out.

During all this time, the captain had the boat at maximum depth heading into a safer area ahead dead slow. If a crew member wasn't on watch, he was in his rack minimizing his oxygen use. We were rigged for silent running, which meant that unnecessary conversation and other noise-generating activities were stopped. Any necessary conversation between compartments was carried by sound-powered telephone or messenger. In one stupid stunt of mine I wanted to come up out of the sonar room, which is below the stern dive plane station. The sailor standing the stern planes watch had to stand on the hatch cover. During normal conditions, when you wanted to come up, you pressed a buzzer, which caused the sailor to move, allowing the hatch to be lifted, and you could then climb the ladder out of the room below. You guessed it. I pressed the buzzer. A tap with my hand on the hatch would have been sufficient. Under the silent running conditions, it would have been heard easily. The problem with the buzzer was that it was tied soundwise to the ship's hull, allowing the noise to be transmitted out into the surrounding sea, exposing the boat to possible detection. It was not a smart thing to do. I knew it as soon as I did it too. When I came out of the hatch, none other than the executive officer of the boat was standing the control room watch. His quiet comment to me was, "If I weren't an officer, I'd call you a noisy son of a bitch!" As a twenty-year-old previous landlubber from Montana, I understood the message, and to this day, I am aware of my surroundings and what the conditions of operation are. That was one of life's fundamental messages. Boy! Was I glad I got an A in beer drinking.

In the final hours of our submerged getaway, the amount of oxygen in the air would not sustain the lighting of a match. The match would just glow through its effort to flame then die. Actually, that was one of our own little tests we performed on the atmospheric conditions inside the boat as time progressed.

The atmosphere in the boat at this time was very warm, the air felt dry, and, frankly, it stunk. Kind of like the first time you entered an attic room during a hot summer that had been shut for over a year. There was not much action or talking going on amongst the crew then. Three days under such conditions can seem like weeks when you're working on each new breath. Finally, after a passive sonar search around, the captain ordered the boat to periscope depth for look around. Finding nothing, he surfaced the boat. I tell you, the first grasp for air from the outside through the ventilation ducts for each of us was deep, and there was an exhilarating coolness about the air as it entered our lungs. After surfacing, we proceeded toward port a couple days' sail away.

In major contrast, on the nuclear boat, we had oxygen generators and CO_2 scrubbers in addition to the emergency oxygen and CO_2 absorbent. The air quality was never a problem. In fact, the only major reason a nuke boat would have to come back to port is because the crew ate all the food on board. Also, it needed to surface only before entering port; otherwise, it could stay submerged again until the food ran out.

USS *Permit* SSN594

Okay, back to the subject of moves. I'm counting all the moves the navy had me do to make my claim. I met Jean in Saratoga. I was attending a special naval training school just outside of the town. It was the kind of school that required us sailors to wear civilian clothes and live in apartments in town. How I met her is interesting, and I'll get into that later—well, I guess I can do it now.

Jean's apartment was about a block and a half away from mine and down around the corner. Jean would walk past my apartment coming from Lake Avenue after work some days. It was summertime, so it was a nice warm time to sit on the porch, studying deeply about reactor theory and operation. I would be out on the front porch early in the day concentrating on why a neutron was so effective in causing radioactive fission, resulting in a release of heat energy that heated water for steam generation so that turbines could be driven to propel the boat through the sea. You have to look up from this kind of a technical manual periodically when you're dealing with this stuff. Coincidentally, I looked up one day, and my eye caught Jean approaching. So as not to appear staring, I kept my head positioned in the reading mode and did my scanning with rapid up-and-down eye movement. She glanced my way as she passed and continued on her way. I watched as she moved away. I saw her turn left at the end of my block.

The next day Mother Nature took my side and started a downpour about the time Jean neared the porch steps. Quickly I invited her up onto the porch. She took refuge from the rain, and we talked about incidental stuff until the rain stopped. Then she went on to her apartment. It was easier to say hi after that as she passed by. It wasn't until later at a navy party in Ballston Spa that the relationship began to grow.

There were two other sailors sharing the house I lived in. They too met local girls during our stay. One of the girls happened to be a friend of Jean's. When the word went out about the party, Jean's friend encouraged her to come to the party to "meet Richard!" She came. As one of the sailors opened the door to greet new party comers, I got a glimpse of who was at the door. I jumped up and immediately took Jean under my guidance. We began our relationship at that moment, and it has continued for more than fifty years.

2

Having the moving technique down pat meant you developed a box-storage mentality such that your things came out of a box only when they were needed. And, as with most people, over time you collect a lot of stuff that never comes out of the box after each move. So, as I said, I have all these boxes. By the way, the house we're in now is our final house. I retired in 2004. So the boxes should stay in their current locations until I get to them.

Now I have to clarify the "final house" comment before I go on. Since I became a reasoning person (questionable characteristic to some who know me), many years ago I used to say I am going to head out in a certain direction in life to find my future in that direction because, I concluded, that's where I should go. Well, it never ever worked out that way even after I married Jean. The direction I actually took, though, did turn out to be a rather interesting one, and upon reflection, I couldn't have made a better choice if I tried. So my saying that this house is our final house—well, let's not shut the door on that one. When you think about it, tomorrow is such a fascinating day despite the fact that it never comes to be because by the time you get to tomorrow, it's already today. But even so, it is a new day even if it is today. Not like Bill Murray's in *Groundhog Day*, though.

Jean and I started to travel together when the navy transferred me to a new construction submarine out on the West Coast after we got married in December of 1960. We never stopped traveling and moving until we retired to our current house. The new construction boat was nuclear powered, the one I talked about before. By this time I had spent most of my initial naval duty in schools with a three-month tour of the area around Japan on a diesel boat.

Jean and I spent our formative marriage years out in California. That meant that we were 1,500 miles from my parents and 3,000 miles from hers. We were also in the navy. Yes, we both were. I was official. She was by default. And this is the same girl who did not like the city. Yet she had no problem moving across the United States with someone she married after a three-month love affair. Incidentally, over fifty years later, the love affair continues. But you have to ask the question, "What caused Jean to leap to the West Coast and yet not stay a couple hundred miles to the south in New York City?" So began our family. And so began our travels together too.

My diesel was a WWII boat out of Pearl Harbor, which I was on prior to marrying Jean. The diesel boat took me to places I only read about. Before I could be assigned to the boat or any boat for that matter, the navy sent me to submarine school in New London, Connecticut. However, before I went to sub school, I went to an electronics school on the West Coast. Then after I was assigned to my diesel boat, I attended a special sonar school in preparation for going on a long patrol out into the Pacific Ocean. Sounds confusing, I suppose, all those schools. Even after I reported aboard my diesel boat, my schooling continued in submarine systems and procedures. And before I could go to my next school, which was nuclear power school, I had to qualify as a submariner on the diesel boat. I had to earn my dolphins. That meant that I had to learn the function and operation of every system on the boat because you never knew where you would be in the boat when an emergency arose. For example, I had to be able to trim the boat after a dive by moving seawater between trim tanks with the trim pump. To trim a boat means to level the boat fore and aft and make it vertical port to starboard. I had to be able to operate the fire control panel. I had to be able to know how to load a torpedo into the tube and make it ready for shooting. As a final test, after passing the formal test on the boat, I had to drink a glass of whiskey into which my new dolphins had been dropped. I had to finish the drink with them between my teeth. Like I said, for me, I was seeing the world and getting educated during the process. By the way, I drank my dolphins in a bar in Yokosuka, Japan.

I was discharged from the navy in February of 1964 at San Diego, California. I didn't need to spend time in the reserve because I had spent six years active, which exempted the reserve time. Two weeks before my discharge I moved from my boat to a barracks for sailors on their way out. Leaving my boat was not too difficult. I had put in my time. I remember standing on the pier with my duffel bag looking at the place where I had spent three years of my life. The topside watch was doing his thing, which was not much. Being tied up at the sub base made the watch somewhat mundane, with the most important duty being watching for the captain of the boat as he came and went. It was much different in Hong Kong harbor on my diesel boat where we anchored offshore and had two topside watches, one at the sail and one aft on deck just above the stern planes, each carrying automatic rifles.

I've tried to compare the two boats, trying to decide which one I enjoyed being on the most. When I was on the diesel, I was new to the navy and the world. On the nuke, I was a qualified submariner highly trained in nuclear power. My six years in the navy consisted of three years of school and three years of sea duty. Moving through the six years, I just went from one experience to the next, with each one piling its exposure on top the previous one.

The diesel boat was less complicated. It saw action in World War II. My book on submarines says she was able to damage a cruiser with a couple of torpedoes somewhere in the Philippine islands area of the Pacific. When I reported aboard in 1959, it was homeported in Pearl Harbor, doing routine patrol duties in the Pacific. I'd been to schools, but I was now going to join the real navy. I was becoming part of a crew of sailors whose job it was to help protect the shores of the United States. As a twenty-year-old, my naiveté was just beginning to wear off. Like I say, I began my life in East Helena, Montana, where the water was neither salty nor vast as the ocean I had flown over to get to this boat. Montana water has beautiful trout that taste delicious when dipped in flour, salt, and pepper then fried in a pan over a campfire.

Before I continue (and this will be a habit in this story, I'm afraid), there is an observation to be made about the formal schooling you get as you grow up compared to the eyes-on schooling you get as you travel to the places that were discussed in the books you were assigned to read in school. My high school education took place between 1953 and 1956. Junior high school took care of the freshman year. My navy schooling, training, and performance fits in between 1958 and 1964. The Cold War was in full swing. The politics of the time and the media made sure we students knew the terribleness of the Union of Soviet Socialist Republics. I don't recall studying about Russia as a country by itself—maybe we did. In any event, I had a very negative view of Russia stemming from its identity as the center of the Soviet, at least until I had a chance to go there.

In the mid-nineties I got my chance to go and, in fact, was able to work in Russia. The company I worked for had a contract to help start private land development so that Russian families could buy houses on time **à** la America. One of the sites being developed was in southern Siberia. I had an occasion to travel to the site for a review of the progress, a flight that carried our group over many time zones. Our office manager there was Russian. He took the opportunity to invite some of us to his home for dinner. He was still living in a Soviet-style apartment building. It was at this dinner that I discovered that I knew very little about the Russian people. My high school history class did not tell me about the strong extended-family structure that existed there. I was amazed at the respect given the elderly. More to the point, I was amazed at what had not been taught me. Perhaps it was just me not listening—do you think? We'll see.

When I returned to Moscow after my trip to Siberia, I took a closer look at what was happening in Russia since the fall of Communism. The story goes that the day after the fall, the mayor of Moscow began the reconstruction of the Russian Orthodox Cathedral, Christ the Savior, on a 24/7 basis. Stalin had blown it up and finally had a swimming pool constructed in its place. Very few Russians swam in it, I was told. All the time I spent in Russia, the reconstruction was going on. When I left in 1996, the cathedral was well on its way to completion. In fact, part of it was rededicated about the time I left. The work was funded by donations from the people themselves. The work included a gold leaf covering over the dome of the cathedral. This is interesting in that one of the translators we used in our Moscow office, who was an important person in the teaching of the beauties of Communism to children during the period of domination, made a revealing comment to me. She was in an organization called the Komsomol. We used to have discussions about the changes that had occurred since the fall of the Soviets. She remarked during one of these discussions that a central principle of the party to be taught to the children was that the state was God, and therefore the people should look to the state for their needs. Apparently, she and the organization were not too successful. One of the outcomes of my dinner in Siberia was that I saw how much devotion to the Russian Orthodox Church every member of the family reflected. The apartment had religious icons on many shelves.

Another enterprising action taken by Stalin was to have five replicas of the Wrigley building in Chicago erected in Moscow. He liked the way the building looked in a photograph, I guess. One of the company persons I worked with had an apartment in one of them. I wasn't impressed with their apartment, nor was he. The building I lived in was quite different. It was originally built for the friends of the Communist Party. It had twenty-foot ceilings and a chandelier in every room except the kitchen and bathroom.

The wood trim detail in each room was outstanding. The building common areas—i.e., the stairwells, elevators, the entrances, etc., were the same—however, as the Wrigley replicas. It was the practice in those days, and I'm sure in days previous, that the common area of each building was the responsibility of the municipal government to maintain and keep clean. Many times as I returned to my apartment at the end of my workday I would have to be careful after entering the building not to step in piles of dirt or on a homeless person using the area as his resting place and other personal needs. I was glad that my apartment's outside door was of a metal construction. I took the elevator up to my floor once but decided it was better to walk up the flight of stairs than to risk getting stuck between floors. And then there were the steps one has to ascend or descend. Here in the United States, when you use a stairway, you are able to move in a rhythmic motion up or down because the step sizes are uniform. You can get your legs moving without regard to skipping a step or two or losing your balance. Not so in the common areas of my apartment building or most of the buildings constructed during the Communist era. I don't recall a stairway in Moscow or the outlying towns where large concrete apartment complexes were erected for the people that regular step heights were present. This may sound like a silly observation, but it speaks to the attitude of those responsible for infrastructure construction during the heady days of Stalin, Khrushchev, Brezhnev, and their party's concern for the proletariat. (Back in June of 2012, the twenty-seventh to be exact, I happened to be watching TV and saw a report on the Thirty-Sixth Street subway stairway in Brooklyn, New York, which had one step slightly higher than the rest of the steps, causing many riders emerging from below to stumble.)

There was another project that my company had in Russia that tells the story of governmental attention to detail. This project was the result of an agreement between President Clinton and President Yeltsin to help get the Russian military out of the Baltic States. Our project was to build apartments for the retiring military officers coming out of Latvia, Estonia, and Lithuania. We either built from the ground up or took over the construction of buildings already in progress.

I took a picture of one of our project buildings in progress where one-half was constructed under Communist rule and the other half was being completed by us. I was able to take a shot of an inside corner of the building exterior that showed the two construction methods used coming together. The obvious difference was on our side, where the bricks were laid straight and level with uniform mortar thickness between the bricks. The irony here is that we used the same contractor who built the other side.

Moscow Apartment Building Construction Differences

In defense of the Russian contractor, I must relate a story told to me by another contractor about his performance during Communist rule. Each contractor building apartments was required to build so many square meters of apartment space within a prescribed time, a time set by the local party commissar. During one period, he said, he fell behind in completing his quota. The local commissar took him to task for his failure. The contractor admitted his poor performance and offered as his punishment not to take his vacation that year. The commissar felt that was sufficient and allowed the contractor to continue building apartments. The quality of the work was not a factor.

In another box, I found my first letter to Jean, which I had written just after getting settled in at the Aerostar Hotel in Moscow, a temporary living quarters until I found an apartment. The letter was dated November 5, 1994 and begins, "My Love."

> Here I am after one week in Moscow, Russia, sitting in my hotel room listening to CNN and trying to see the laptop computer screen through the sunlight coming in the window. The temperature outside is right at the freezing point. I've spent the past week trying to overcome jet lag. We work from 9:00 in the morning until 6:00 at night, which made it more difficult to do anything after work except hit the sack following dinner. I seem to be adjusted now.
>
> Moscow is in better shape than what you and I saw in St. Petersburg. The city is in better repair, though a lot of work still needs to be done. My hotel room is comparable to an average room in the states. It reminds me of a Holiday Inn-type room. The food is OK but expensive. Last night I had a New York steak and two glasses of wine. $47.00. My breakfasts cost $18.00 regardless of what I eat. A half liter of water is $3.50. I try to drink most of my water at the office since it's provided there. I haven't touched the tap water except to take a shower in.
>
> When I arrived at the airport and proceeded through passport control and customs, it reminded me of when you and I went through in Saudi Arabia.

I spent an hour in the passport control line, which, I was told, was short since only our plane and one other was passing through at that time. After successfully running the gauntlet, I started looking for my contact, who was to get me to the right hotel. I must have walked around the airport twenty times over the next hour looking for a sign with my name on it. The only thing I was able to accomplish was to look like a person who needed a taxi. I was inundated with offers from taxi drivers; I finally got fed up with the onslaught and went to a reservation desk and got a hotel and a taxi to take me there. The person who said he came to pick me up didn't use a sign or wander around looking for me. I even tried to have an announcement made, but each time I contacted the person who makes them, she hung up on me, I think because she didn't understand my language. Well, all's well that ends well—I guess. It proves to me again that you must take care of yourself.

The project is an interesting one. The U.S. is funding the construction of housing for returning Russian officers from the Baltic States, Latvia, Lithuania, Estonia, and other areas they occupied during the Communist years. My company is the construction manager for the project where contractors from either the U.S. or Russia or a combination of both will do the actual construction. There was large response to the project from over two hundred companies. If I were to stay on here, I might be traveling to each site.

I sure would get close to the Russian people that way. Maybe I'll get to learn a second language, yet! [I was on temporary assignment at this time, but I eventually became a permanent part of the project team.]

I have found the Russian contractors who were successful in getting their proposals accepted to be just like any other contractor around the world. They know their local situation and how their world works. The dollar speaks loudly. On the other hand, the quality of what they will build will be comparable to a typical tenement house in New York City which has been lived in for the past thirty years.

There are only seven of us here, including me. The rest of the project people are either Russian or Finn. I'm always impressed on how people from different countries can work together when they want to or when their governments decide to let them. Sometimes I wonder if governments would just leave the people alone more progress would be made in what the people want, which is just to be able to do what they want and be happy. I remember the line from a song that says, "even Russians love their children."

Russian rush hour traffic is something else. The driving concept is "every driver for himself." At intersections, grid lock is the norm. When the traffic light changes to red, the cars continue to pass into the intersection, preventing the cars with the green light to go through. It becomes a contest of which driver has the nerve to stick his car's front end into the oncoming traffic pattern and cause a break in it. Then it becomes a grid lock from the cross direction. You may remember some of the traffic in Rome or Jakarta, which are comparable, but not as bad.

Anybody who is driving by can become a taxi driver for the moment. If we need a taxi to get back to the hotel, we stand by the street and hold an arm out. Anybody can stop. You open the door and negotiate a price to the hotel. We have a person who speaks a little Russian, and he does the negotiation. We go in groups to make it easier and safer. We do OK.

We have a laundry service which comes to the office and picks up our clothes. It advertises as a laundry like those in the U.S. Looking at what they've done for others, it looks like they do alright. They are inexpensive also. One dollar per shirt.

The weather has been rainy since I arrived except for the last two days, which have been cold, and some snow has fallen, though none has remained on the ground. Like I said, today is cold, clear, and sunny.

This is all I know for now. I'll get this letter out today, if I can. Otherwise, it will be on Tuesday as Monday is a Russian Holiday—Revolution Day.

I love and miss you. Sometimes I wonder why we are apart so much. I don't have a good answer except that the work path I chose does that to us. One day…

The PS to my letter was, "The *Moscow Times* [November 4, 1994], according to the cartoon I've cut out and enclosed, has already recognized my ability to achieve great things!" The cartoon was a Gary Larson's *The Far Side* with the caption, "By secretly working out for many months, Irwin became the envy of all the 98-pound weaklings." The cartoon showed Irwin standing on a weight scale with one of three observers pointing to the indicated weight of ninety-nine pounds. It was a great feeling to know that Mr. Larson acknowledged I had world appeal.

The Far Side by Gary Larson

3

Okay, so here we are now in Connecticut. I'm the only person, I think, that retired into the state, lending some legitimacy to those who have questioned my reasoning ability.

I actually began my travels as a child moving from East Helena, Montana, to Whitefish, Montana, and then on to a small lake town in Washington state. The reason I bring this up is the move to Whitefish. My mother and father moved us from a small house in the small town of East Helena to a small log cabin on a farm outside of Whitefish. I've told this story to our children and reminded them of the story many times. My father had secured a job as an electrician on the railway that passed through Whitefish on a line that went from Seattle to Chicago. It was a helper position, so there was not much salary, just potential for advancement. (Had he not gotten sick back in the mid-sixties, I was told he would have moved up to the position of general electrical foreman for the western division of the railroad.) The rent for the cabin was ten dollars per month. My three brothers, my sister, and I spent the winter of 1946 there. My younger and third brother was born the fall before that winter. I told this story to our children as an example of what it takes sometimes to get from here to there.

Montana winters are not the easiest to endure. The cold air would keep the snow so dry that it would pelt your face like a sandstorm as you did your outside things. It was an awesome sight to see the dry snow move slowly like a snake down the street in front of the moving car in the early morning sun. It was a frightful sight to see the snow angrily move straight across the road when the wind was colder and brisker. Sometimes it was difficult to see the road even though the sun was brightly shining. The snow would blow across the road, coming off the open fields at a low level barely a foot off the pavement, causing the road to disappear from your vision. The barbed wire fence along the side of the road became your reference. The assumption was that the fence paralleled the road. And most of the time, it did.

Now the logs of a log cabin are neither uniform in circumference nor smooth on their surface. To take care of the resultant gaps between the logs stacked lengthwise one on top of the other to make the outside wall as well as the inside one, a grout mixture was trawled in between the logs. Unfortunately, over time, the grout would loosen up and sometimes fall out, leaving a small hole to the outside. Our cabin was old. Also, the front door was a construction of several one-inch thick boards about eight inches wide nailed to cross pieces at the top and bottom with a diagonal piece nailed between the cross pieces.

There were only two rooms with a small storage area off one of the rooms in our cabin. The larger room was used for a kitchen at one end, a living room at the other, and a bedroom at night for us three boys. We slept three across in a trundle bed that was our couch during the day. My younger brother had a bassinette. My sister slept in the storage room. There was a small wood-burning stove toward the kitchen side on which my mother used to cook and which was also used to heat the cabin. We had no running water in the house. I or one of my brothers—or my mother, if we weren't around—had to carry water from a well located in the farmer's backyard about four hundred feet away. No running water meant no inside toilet either. That was out behind the cabin in a clump of trees. It was a "two-holer." Each hole was a different size to accommodate different-sized people, I guess.

As I mentioned above, Montana winters are not always easy to endure. We would sometimes awaken in the morning after an unusually windy and snowy night and see a line of snow on the floor extending inward about two feet from a corner of the door. Or snow would be built up on the inside of one the logs where some of the grout had been pushed out by the swirling wind. My mother would already be up stoking the stove to get the heat going. She also needed to get the fire started to melt the ice that had formed in the water pail overnight.

Living on the farm meant that grocery stores, gas stations, and other stores were in town. I think we were about five miles out of town. The road past the house was a dirt road. There is one day that sticks vividly in my mind about the road and our car. Our car was a 1938 Chevy sedan. In this car, the windshield wipers were moved by a small motor operated by the vacuum system in the car's engine. The motors were mounted inside just above the windshield with the wiper blade attached to a shaft penetrating the metal rim of the windshield. One very windy, cold, snowy morning, my mother had to take the car into town to have some repairs made to the car. I went with her. The wipers were working intermittently as she started out. And, to complicate her drive, the defroster was not working well enough to keep the frost from building up on the windshield. She had to keep wiping the fog buildup off from the inside of the windshield. After a short while on the road, the wiper froze in the middle of the windshield. Returning to the cabin was out of the question, apparently, because my mother continued toward town. But, to continue, my mother had to roll the door window down and stick her head out in order to see the road ahead. As I sit here now, I reflect on that time when I could see her face turning red from the cold wind blowing on it. Her lips were pursed as she tried to maintain her vision. Her eyes became mere slits in her head to shield them. Even as a child, I remember feeling her pain as she continued driving into town. We made it, finally. The car got fixed, and we returned home.

Funny thing, I don't remember being concerned about my situation. As an eight-year-old I was enjoying all that was going on. I'm sure I got cold and caused my mother problems just because of my age. I was eight years old. I do remember my mother taking care of us, making sure we didn't suffer too much, though. As a matter of fact, all through my growing-up life, my mother saw to my welfare. (I truly believe that God gives every mother the capability to master any obstacle placed in front of her. Mothers are the greatest gift to mankind! Sadly, though, some mothers have forgotten this.)

Before that winter started, I was employed for a dollar a day by a local farmer during the fall haying period to drive a team of horses that pulled hay into a barn via a trolley system. The job had been offered to my older brother, but he had other plans, so my mother suggested I do it. I was a second grader at the time. Each morning I would walk about a mile down the road to the next farm and be home around four in the afternoon. Made fifteen dollars that fall.

Later on, as I've said, when I had my own family, I would use the cabin as a tool to explain to our kids why I felt that their discomfort on a particular issue was not too convincing.

East Helena was just across the railroad tracks from a lead smelter. Every night a worker, maybe more than one, with a large mallet would walk the catwalks that surrounded the very tall smoke stack at various levels pounding the side of the stack in a rhythmic pattern of blows that sent out a low frequency similar to a bass drum. Every twenty seconds or so the sound would echo out over the town throughout the night. You got used to it. This pounding action was necessary to loosen the particulate material caught in the exhaust gases from the smelting process of the lead and collecting on the inside of the stack and let it fall for collection at the bottom. The smelter was the reason we had to move—because of its effect on my father's health.

Now my father was a laborer at the smelter. Also, he never went past the tenth grade in high school. Having to leave his job presented him a real problem. He had to provide for four children, complicating his situation a bit more. To top it off, he decided to become an electrician. He decided to resolve his situation by taking a correspondence course in electricity before looking for another job. Let me try to put this in perspective as I see it.

I put sixteen years into public schools and three years in navy schools. The four college years actually took around eight years because I had to work and go evenings after I got out of the navy. But overall, I progressively built on each previous year of education. Conversely, my father stopped after his tenth year, got married, started a family, and worked as a laborer. As a minimum, learning about electricity requires an understanding of math, at least up to the algebra level. You need the ability to grasp component relationships such as how voltage, current, and resistance concepts interact. You need a good command of the technical word usage of the English language or at least the ability to use a technical dictionary. Obviously, my father had these qualities because he mastered electricity as a discipline and the practical application of its principles. He already had an excellent work ethic, which was as important in his day as knowing which was the hot wire and which one was the neutral. To top all this off, my father was a self-taught banjo player, good enough to play in a local group that included my mother as a piano player. They played thirties and forties music, mostly ragtime. I have never been surprised at what my father could do. I used to help him rewire houses and go with him when he was called to work in the evening. Fond memories for me.

Also, across the tracks from our house was a baseball diamond. It may have been the smelter's recreation field. I was too young to care about who owned it. What I do remember is the game that was played between the House of David and the Harlem Globetrotters. The members of the House of David team all had beards as I recall. And they were extremely fast base runners. A hit that seemed to me to be a single was turned into a double on speed alone. The House of David won. Other than the little school down the street where I first went to, that's about all I remember about the town. Well, there was this bar across the street from our house. I had a friend who lived down past that bar. I would go to his house and play for a while then return home. One time, as I was returning home, a man was going toward the bar after getting out of his pickup truck. That's all he was doing, just walking to the bar. Apparently, I didn't see it that way because I took one look at him and his pickup and ran screaming all the way home. To this day I don't know why I reacted that way. Well, I do remember my mother and I hiding on the stairway going upstairs one day.

4

Sifting through another box from the closet, I found a myriad of papers, plastic ID cards, and small pieces of paper with writing on them. Inside a small par avian envelope, the kind that has the red-and-blue stripes around each edge, was a partial piece of a blue airline napkin with writing on it. Based on what I wrote, I was flying to Russia on my first trip to a new job. It read, "As I fly over the land I have only read about in my history books, I sit in awe of it as its past rises to greet me. Budapest 1956, Berlin 1948, Poland 1981." That quote describes a lot of recent history. In a sense I was recalling some of the high points in the ultimate demise of Communism in 1989. The Hungarian Uprising, the Berlin Airlift, and the declaration of martial law in Poland. I always wanted to go to Russia after the fall, but I think I was also apprehensive about the trip. I really didn't know what to expect. After a lifetime of being told that the USSR was our enemy, it was somewhat disconcerting to be going to a project inside Russia that was being promoted by the United States. But that's what we Americans do.

The project I was going to was the apartment construction project. We had several sites across western Russia from Sochi on the Black Sea to Kaliningrad near the Baltic Sea. There was another one in Stari Oscol and one up north in Novgorod as I recall. There was a couple more whose names I can't recall. It was an interesting experience when we took one of the beneficiaries around his completed apartment to have a look at what he was going to receive. He was amazed that it was totally complete and that all the fixtures were in place and working. Tears came to his eyes as he took in what was going to be his and as something to own. Getting picked up from the airport in Sochi in a Mercedes 600SL with bulletproof windows and an armored-up chassis was an experience too. On the ground, Russia was a struggling new government with one foot in the future and the other dragging; trying to remain in the past. When I was in Siberia, our office manager was required by the local KGB agent to write out my itinerary for my time there. So we did. I forgot what we wrote, but it wasn't what I did. If the agent checked me out, which I doubt, he didn't follow up. I think he had what he needed for his file, and thus his life was complete for the day.

I found a lot of contradictions in Russia during my time there. I hold the opinion that Moscow was not a good reflection of the real Russian people. Each time I traveled outside the city I saw single-dwelling homes, some with people tending small gardens. Some of the houses had intricately designed roof eaves boards, which told me that all was not conformance to the equality standards of the Communist Party. On one occasion I accompanied our project manager to Kaliningrad for a meeting with one of our Russian contractors for a status on progress. Before the meeting started, I did a visual review of the various pictures hanging on the walls of company president's office. I noticed a very appealing painting on the back wall behind his desk. It was of a house located amongst a group of broad-leafed trees. I commented to the president on its beauty just before the meeting started. He responded that his daughter had painted it. I remarked that he should tell his daughter what a good painting it was. After the meeting was over, we had proceeded back to our hotel to prepare for the return trip to Moscow. The following morning, I received a knock on my room door. Upon answering, the person who had knocked handed me a wrapped package. In the package was the picture. I was surprised but was told that it was a tradition in Russia that when a compliment is given on such things, you are offered it as a result. Had I known this tradition, I might have been more discreet in my words. But now, the painting hangs on our wall in the loft.

In contrast, what represented the party was the massive number of prefabricated concrete apartment complexes with the uneven common area stairs. What represented the people in my mind were these houses and the private gardens alongside the commune gardens. The contrast in the gardens was impressive in just the color of the plants. Such rich colors in the private gardens were amazing. And I've already mentioned the rebuilding of the cathedral in Moscow, which is another representation of the Russian people.

I'll mention just a couple more examples, and then I'll go look at another piece of paper or a tag of some sort in the box. In contrast to the comment our translator, who had been the head of Komsomol in Moscow, made about God and the state, I used to go to Mass in a church that was a stone's throw from the KGB building. I would take the subway from the station close to my apartment to the station close to Lubyanka Square in the center of Moscow, which brought me to the surface close by the building. Walking to the church took me along one side of the building around to the back, and then I would cross the street and go up a smaller street a couple hundred feet to a nondescript building that did not look anything like a church, least of all a Catholic one. But inside, there was no doubt. It looked like any church I'd seen and attended Mass in wherever in the world I had been. The building was old, though, and, except for an apparent cleaning routine, had not been kept up. The center aisle sagged down noticeably due to, I suppose, weakened or rotting floor supports, and there was no heat during winter. The priest would wear a heavy coat under his vestments during the sacrifice of the Mass. The church was always packed at every Mass I attended. In fact, I had to get there early if I wanted to have a seat. There was a side altar on the right side of the church where the Blessed

Virgin's statue was stationed. A long line of Russians were always standing silently waiting for their turn to kneel at the railing. As Mass proceeded on a very cold day, there would be a faint collection of the vapors from each person's breath rising. Sometimes the organ would break down or squeal out a discordant note. The singer, always of Bolshoi quality, would continue in spite of the organ's antics. The people attending spanned the ages of children to the elderly. I volunteered to do the readings at some of the Masses. It was obvious to me that Lenin, through Brezhnev, was not able to erase what the Russian people held in their hearts.

I would always sit on the right side of the church. That was the Blessed Virgin's side, and I was partial. On the other side I always saw two or more Sisters of the Missionaries of Charity, Mother Teresa's order. I occasionally had a few extra dollars in my pocket, some of which I was able to give to one of the sisters at the end of a Mass. One day they asked if I would like to visit their convent and see what they were doing with the money I gave them. I jumped at the chance. The sisters took care of the homeless and destitute Russians that mostly came from the streets of Moscow. I remember that six sisters were handling around forty men at the time I visited.

5

I walked to work in Moscow every day. Winter through fall. As I walked down the boulevard on any day going back to my apartment, I would pass by several people standing on the building side of the sidewalk close to an intersection or next to the walkway that went under the boulevard. Some were even in the underground walkway. These people were selling single packages of cigarettes, a few vegetables, a set of silverware, or some other small item. Some of the people were elderly ladies dressed in their mink fur coats if it was winter. They were the ones who were selling the family heirlooms.

One day I watched a man trying to decide which way to cross the intersection. He stood there looking first one way then the other. He looked to be about forty-five. His confusion was all over his face. Unfortunately, I saw him later during a cold January day, lying on his side on a park bench with his face away from view. He was dead. Two plainclothes police were standing by the bench, apparently waiting for the vehicle that would take him away.

I watched the Russian youth on the streets. Practically every one of them was wearing American-style jeans. I don't know if the jeans were made in America, but those wearing them acted like they were.

There was another Russian lady working as a translator for us. We were having difficulty organizing some of our work. I remarked to her one day that maybe I should write a procedure on the process. She replied that yes, I should do that, and then we should put it in the same place where all the others that the commissars of the past had created and usually ended up. I speculated on her comment for a while and decided that perhaps a better way to solve our problem was in order other than use of the circular file.

Upon reflection, I saw the four different scenarios above as what Russia was facing as its future unfolded. It was like one day Communism was the rule, and the next there was no rule. For some—for a lot, maybe, because the state controlled all—it meant that without the control, having to make decisions became an uncertain activity like the man at the street corner. The women having to sell their heirlooms reflected an unpreparedness for the new way, and the youth, always ready to extend their reality, represented an effort to take advantage of the new day. At the same time, attendance at church played into the value given to the culture as it matures. The result was a mixed cultural bag that plagues and also maybe gives hope to Russia today.

Went back to the box. I pulled out a picture that showed St. Basil's Church at the back of Moscow's Red Square. This picture has major significance for me because it was showing a relationship that could have been developing between the United States and the Russia post-Communism of the USSR.

July 4, 1995, was a memorable celebration of Independence Day for me. I was in Russia. I have this picture I took at Moscow's Red Square. We had gotten word from the US Embassy that a parade was going to be held in Red Square to celebrate the day. Several of us took the subway to the square to watch. We came on to the Square from a street opposite St. Basil's Church and away from the Kremlin Wall. Looking slightly left across the Square next to the wall was Lenin's tomb. I had taken the tour to see him in his glass-covered box. He looked kind of red. The story is that the embalmers screwed up, and their efforts caused his skin to show a reddish color while "lying in state." The tomb designers tried to minimize the redness with lights, but it didn't work.

As we continued to walk toward St. Basil's, we heard the music of a military marching band approaching. Most squares, such as the Red and Tiananmen in China, being as large as they are, have the appearance of a raised center so that standing at one end, you are not able to see the other. So when the sound of the marching band playing, if you will, "Stars and Stripes Forever" preceded its approach, I looked toward the sound but saw only the American eagle stop a flagpole that carried the Stars and Stripes rising as it moved to the center of the Square. What an awesome sight it was! Then it got better. The marching band was an American Air

Force band, in uniform no less! This was even better than when I watched the Ford Crown Victoria leading the parade of the Communist Party regulars down Tverskoy Boulevard and the traffic police carrying Motorola radios. Anyway, I was overcome with emotion. The significance of this band marching down Red Square past Lenin's tomb and the Ford spoke volumes about the status of the world in 1995. It spoke volumes about the reaction of the Russian people to their new status. I was glad I was there.

US Air Force Marching Band on Red Square

Ford Crown Victoria Leading Communist Parade in Moscow

I went back to the box again and began sifting through its contents. I found a patch that was given to the NATO military when they became the stabilizing force after the Bosnian War. It has the letters IFOR vertically on the shield-shaped patch with the equivalent in Cyrillic on the right side. IFOR stands for "Implementation Force." Six months after IFOR set up shop in Sarajevo, I was one of six people from my company to go in by car to set our shop up to help begin the reconstruction of Bosnia's infrastructure. I was still in Russia when the Dayton Accords was signed in Paris on December 14, 1995, which provided for NATO to come in and try maintaining peace. As I was doing my work in Russia, I kept looking at Bosnia wondering how two longtime neighbors, one Bosnian and one Serb, living in Sarajevo could suddenly, one day, turn and shoot at each other with intent to kill. All the news reporting wasn't making sense. Of course, I was not up on my history of the area; otherwise, I might have understood. I wanted to know the answer, so the first opportunity to volunteer for the project that might come up, I made sure my name was in the hat. The position I ended up having put me in direct contact with a lot of the local people of the local contractors. I was assigned the project procurement manager. They gave me an earful. My ultimate trips around Bosnia gave me an eyeful.

A Bosnian who worked with us commented one day that until the war, he considered himself a Bosnian. After the start, he began to see himself more as a Muslim because the position all Bosnians were put in by the Serbs, who were fighting "Muslims and Croatians," not Bosnians.

As it turns out, if you draw a north-south line on a map through Sarajevo, you have essentially divided east from west. This line was drawn for me when I visited Zagreb, Croatia, for a business meeting and asked the question of a Croatian. He explained that over the centuries the line moved east or west, plus or minus a hundred miles, depending on which culture was dominant at the time. National interests, religious interests, and cultural interests kept the line moving to and fro until Yugoslavia came to be. All these interests were suppressed by Marshal Tito and his form of Communism. As long as Yugoslavia existed, the Bosnian, the Serb, and the Croat lived in the same neighborhood—in Sarajevo at least. Then Yugoslavia fell. The nationalism, the religion, and the cultures returned to prominence—and so did the conflicts. As it turned out, the Croats and the Bosnians appeared to have resolved their differences sufficiently, but the Serbs did not with either. Eventually, a federation was established between the two when the war broke out with the Serbs.

Like I said, I was still in Russia when Bosnia was beginning to settle down. The six of us gathered in Zagreb, Croatia, to begin the drive into Sarajevo, where we would establish our office in an old schoolhouse. We could not drive straight into Sarajevo along the northern autobahn-style four-lane highway. We chose to drive to the Adriatic coast then go south to Ploče and inland thru Mostar to Sarajevo, thinking this route would be much safer than the route closer to Serbia. Serbia had not yet settled down and didn't like what we were doing. In fact, part of our project was to repair some of the infrastructure in the Serb-held area, but they prevented us from doing anything. They always said they would accept the money allocated for the repairs, however. Not something we could do, so their repairs went undone.

I had never driven or even been close to an area devastated by war. It had only been six months since the conflict had stopped, so the damage was still everywhere. After being in

Sarajevo for a while, some of the people told stories of Serb tanks driving down roads blowing holes in houses as they passed by. Some people said further that the destruction was not random but targeted non-Serb houses. On my trip in, I saw many of these houses abandoned along the road and increasingly so the closer we got to Sarajevo. Even the power lines along the highway had their electrical wire removed, preventing the distribution of power to the houses. I also saw home owners already starting to rebuild as we entered Sarajevo. The resilience of victims of war is amazing. On the other hand, watching a person clean up a room whose outside walls have been blown away makes you wonder about the ability to rebuild. On the other hand, part of our infrastructure rebuild project was to put a disassembled coal-fired generator back together so that Sarajevo and its surrounding areas could go from a 10 percent power supply to a 100 percent supply. It was great to see the lights stay on when the generator went online.

War Damage by Serbs outside Sarajevo, Bosnia

For the first few days we stayed in a hotel outside of Sarajevo. It was set in a rural area with a background of low-rising hills covered with grassy open spaces. The tree line was higher up and in some cases followed gullies down toward the level of the hotel but at a distance. There was a road that went up into these hills that we used to do our exercise running each morning. We stayed out of the hills in the late afternoons and evenings. Too many locals were using what sounded like AK-47s for their target practice during that period. My room was on the hillside, and I could look up into the hills for a pleasant view each day. One evening the sound of AK-47s seemed closer than usual. So close that I heard the zing of the bullets going over the hotel. At one point I dropped to the floor because the apparent direction of the bullets seemed to be aimed close to my window. I was never interested in the view after that. After a week or so we moved into Sarajevo to the apartments we rented for the duration.

A few months into the project I had to go to Pale for a meeting with the Serb government head responsible for construction in the Serb-held territory to discuss rebuilding of one of the government buildings there. Pale was the location of the headquarters for the Serbian government in that area. Our project effort was to aid in the reconstruction of the Serbian areas in addition to the Federation-held areas. Our project was to be seen as being fair to both sides. All the two sides had to do was to submit requests for repair to an infrastructure area destroyed by the war. In the Serb's case, however, they just wanted the money, and they would see to it that it was used "appropriately." Thus, my meeting did not go well. It was the Serb's desire to name the contractor to make the repairs and that we would pay whatever it cost. My explanation of the requirements of the American Federal Procurement Regulations left them with little to say except repeating that just giving the money was the better idea. The meeting ended shortly after that exchange. The US government representative attending the meeting with me translated some of the parting words the Serb about me and my adherence to the procurement rules as we left the building.

One day in the routine of the project, I was attending to some paperwork at my desk. We had several Bosnians working in the office, each doing their paperwork as well. The buyer who was on my staff was busy buying material for one of the smaller projects we were doing. Another person was concentrating on a computer database. The office was quiet except for an occasional scuffing noise of a chair being moved or paper going from one spot on a desk to another. Mostly, the office was quiet. Our offices were in an old school building on the ground floor. I sat next to a window at my back. I don't remember what part of the day it was, but all of a sudden I heard a very loud explosion and felt the building shake. I pushed back on my chair and began a ducking motion that was going to take me under my desk. Obviously, I thought, a bomb of some sort had hit close by. My effort was to get under the desk for protection against the next one that was probably on its way. And my being close to a window didn't help my anxiety at all. On my way down to the safety under my desk, I glanced over to see how the Bosnians were moving to protect themselves. No one was moving! They just continued doing their work. With great finesse, I continued to the floor and picked up an imaginary pencil that I could argue I had "dropped" under my desk and sat back up as smoothly as I possibly could. After my recovery, I remarked that the noise I just heard was quite loud. The buyer replied that it was just an earthquake. They happened quite often, she said.

I was amazed that what I took for an explosion barely raised an eyebrow on the Bosnians. They could make out the difference with ease. Upon reflection, I now understood how a person could distinguish a noise that to me was exactly what a bomb would sound like from what it actually was—an earthquake. I had forgotten how I was able to distinguish between noises generated by different operating machines in the engine room of my submarine. Being a reactor operator, my watch station was in the maneuvering room, which was a small room within the engine room. We operated the propulsion systems, the reactor plant systems, and electrical systems from this room. The noise level was muted somewhat by the sound isolation material, but the noises of each machine were still heard. There was a quiescent state of noise mix that I and the other submariners in the room understood as a normal operating engine room. Conversations would be conducted and functions carried out routinely inside the mix. Even when the mix changed due to speed variations or activation of some idle pump to perform an expected or directed operation, it was taken in stride. It was when something happened out of sequence that attention was drawn to a corrective action. That was me in the Sarajevo school building. For the Bosnians, it was an explainable event consistent with their experience. They knew what a bomb sounded like and what an earthquake sounded like.

In a way, it was sad that they didn't act like I did. But my world back home did not include bombs or exploding artillery shells or tank cannon shells or the resultant killing. I guess in any situation in the world, good or bad, life has to go on. You adapt to what you can't control. The Russians did it during the Communist era. Then, at the end of what you can't control, you return as much as possible to what you did before the "troubles" started, as the Irish called their conflict. Unfortunately, with the end of Yugoslavia came the return to the historical differences of the nations now freed. The memories of the old don't go away easily. In that area of the world it turned out that the old memories included a lot of unresolved issues. An example of this memory comes from a story told to me by one of our project people, a scheduler, who had to make a trip to Serbia for a discussion on the use of scheduling software with one of our contractors. Putting a schedule down on paper was risky business during the Communist period as it could be used against you if you miss your goal. But we insisted, so they were conforming.

During the visit the scheduler had dinner with the owner of the Serbian company. As it happens at any dinner, stories were told, opinions given, and revelations made. The owner was lamenting about the way the war had treated his relatives. He remarked that some of his relatives had been captured by the other side and brutally murdered by being thrown down a bottomless pit. As he was speaking, he pulled several photographs out of his shirt pocket and laid them on the table, indicating that these were the relatives done in. The conversation continued a bit longer as the scheduler tried to get more specific about the timing and actual location of the killings, expecting to hear of some location in Bosnia. Finally, the owner exclaimed that he was not talking about the Bosnian War but the Second World War. The culprits were really Croats aligned with the German command. As I said, memories can linger a long time.

I'm not sure that the youth would be as resilient though. Their memories are shorter. If you're born in a war zone, your developing experiences take war as the way things are. Without the older people and parents who care for their children, being there to counsel the youth, I'm not sure what the outcome would be.

During the Bosnian War, the Serbs had the habit of lobbing mortars into various places in Sarajevo during the busy times of the day. They did the same thing, of course, in other towns. Being in Sarajevo, I was able to see the physical results of these attacks. It's an interesting pattern that a mortar makes when it explodes after landing on concrete. The sidewalks in most of Sarajevo were concrete as well as plazas like the one in front of the Catholic Sacred Heart Cathedral. Looking closely you can see a gouging of the concrete that spreads out in fairly straight lines from the point of impact beginning no more than a half-inch deep decreasing to nothing as it moves outward. Their lengths were anywhere from an inch to maybe ten inches out from the center. Occasionally, a gouge would be longer. The center of impact was rounded somewhat but were mostly irregularly shaped. The bottom of the gouge looked spoon shaped in some cases and V-shaped in others. Sometimes the gouge would start several inches out from the center and continue a few more inches. The gouge's shape and size, it seemed, depended on the explosive capability of the mortar coming in and the piece of shrapnel doing the gouging. Despite the gouging in the concrete, most of the shrapnel resulting from the explosion moved in an upward and expanding pattern. You can get an idea of how the shrapnel moves by looking at the base of the buildings along the sidewalks. If the mortar hits close to the building, there will be holes in the brick or wood down low. The holes in the building are higher the farther away the mortar hit. When you inspect the holes in the buildings, you notice that the depth of the penetration goes anywhere from a couple of inches to a scrape. The scrape marks are higher on the wall as they appear to be caused by a glancing contact. The spread of the holes along the wall is a function of the distance from the exploding mortar. Occasionally, I saw pieces of the mortar still in the holes. They varied in size, from a quarter inch to a couple of inches. If you can imagine the mortar as it explodes, the resulting sizes of the pieces comes from the ability of the mortar casing to withstand the blast before it disintegrates. The heat of the explosion also contributes to the shape and size of each piece of shrapnel. Most of the heat of the explosion stays with each piece until it reaches its destination, transferring it to the object that stops the piece. The mortar casing is designed to break into many pieces so that a lot of area is covered as they move outward in a spherical dome like concentration. As I walked down the sidewalk or in the plaza in front of the church, I noticed that several of the patterns had been filled with red-colored material that had been poured in and allowed to solidify. The starkness of the red called to the mind of everyone who saw it what had taken place as the unknowing people were busy walking to their destination for that day when the mortar hit the concrete. And, depending on the distance from the exploding mortar, each person could be unaffected or be hit as the buildings were hit. These red-filled mortar patterns in the concrete are called Sarajevo Roses.

I have a postcard of a viola player in Sarajevo. He's sitting in the middle of the destroyed National Library. He has his viola fixed in its playing position with the bow in his left hand and extending over the strings. However, his right hand is covering his brow and eyes trying to hide the sadness he obviously feels. Behind him, on the floor of the main part of the library, is the rubble from the bombing carried out by the Serbs. The roof is gone. Most of the support columns are damaged. The second-story balcony looks very precarious. I understood his sadness.

Here's a new preconstruction task not found on many construction sites. For each project we awarded, the first action to be taken before anyone could even walk the site to consider what bid they would eventually offer was that the site had to be demined. Our Mine Awareness Training reminded us at the outset of the program that "if it's green, don't walk on it!" By the way, the solid entrenchment of that admonition took a while to abate after I returned from Bosnia. I continued to walk only on roads, driveways, and sidewalks at home until one day I realized what I was doing. I sort of had to purposely take a step on to the lawn to break the pattern of the habit.

In Bosnia—probably everywhere though—it was a sad but somewhat safe observation that wherever children were playing on green, it generally was okay. Unfortunately, it wasn't always a reliable method because of the terrible consequences when children went beyond their area of play. Actually, it was one of the deminer's first actions when surveying a new area to be demined. The children were good sources of information on where mines may have been placed as they might have seen them being put or had played in the area recently with no resultant tragedy. I wondered why I saw boxes of candy and small toys on the shelves when I initially came to visit the deminer's site offices. I also saw how the deminers took care of alerting the children about the possibility of mines in their area of play. A handout had been prepared that used Superman as the person who would come to the aid of children about to enter an area that had mines laying around.

Superman not only came to their aid but took the time to educate and train them in mine avoidance. It was a typical comic book format seen in America.

We had one project to make repairs at a school in Sarajevo. The school had been used as defense position by the Serbs. The demining company we used was called in to demine the school and its grounds. It is not an easy task to demine.

I'm sure everyone has seen an action movie where a character finds himself in a mine field. After freezing his motion, the character slowly bends his knees toward the ground while removing his standard military-issue bayonet-looking knife from its sheath conveniently looped on to his belt. He methodically begins to probe the ground in front of him, carefully inserting the knife at a thirty-degree angle to the surface in a slow motion, ready to cease forward movement if any resistance is felt. He moves forward inch by inch as he heads to safety out of the field. The tension of the scene is enhanced when he makes contact with an object. A closer look reveals a small cylindrical metal pin about six inches from where the knife entered the soil coming in contact with something, sticking up out of the soil but hidden by a leaf. Slowly the leaf is lifted and removed so a better examination can be made. The character has a decision to make: does he stand and carefully step across to continue his trek to safety, or does he change direction and try again?

If he decides to step over, he first has to reach across and continue probing because those who planted the first mine understood the choices needed to be made if the first mine was found. The planter puts a second one in proximity to the first one to catch the guy who chooses to step over. Hence the need to continue probing. But having to reach across the first mine puts the prober at risk. What if he loses his balance? What if the mine is too sensitive and goes off because of the vibrations caused by the motion of the knife poking into the dirt? What if there is a trip mechanism set up to trigger the mine when the knife cuts a fish line staked just beyond the mine?

On the other hand, the character can proceed left or right to make his way to safety. But again, the planter knows this tendency too. So he places another mine on either side of the one found. The planter has all avenues covered now. The only reasonable option for the character now is retreat. On the other other hand, the character can step across a mine that was missed one step back. By turning around and taking a step back the way he had come, the character can step on the mine and be killed.

Well, the director of that movie was sure imaginative. He wasn't going to let the character survive no, matter what. The storyline couldn't do without this kill. All right, let's return to reality. After doing an informational reconnoiter amongst the people in the area, the deminer assigned to the task dons his bomb suit and stands in front of his entry point to begin his intimate massage of the ground. He takes out his standard military-issue bayonet-looking knife from its sheath conveniently looped on to his belt, bends down at the knees, and begins to probe the dirt by inserting the knife at a thirty-degree angle very slowly every inch or so. On his next probe into the dirt, he contacts an object. Looking six inches ahead, he discovers a metal pin sticking out of the dirt. Very carefully he removes the leaf covering the pin so that he can get a better look.

Each time a deminer finds a mine, a decision has to be made whether it can be removed by hand and destroyed at another place or whether it should be destroyed in place. The preference is to destroy in place as it is obviously safer. A small amount of explosive material is placed beside the mine, and then the mine is covered with special blankets that would contain the explosion. This process continues until an assessment is made that the area is 97 percent demined. It is impossible to get to 100 percent confidence level as there could always be one overlooked despite the completeness of the cleaning effort. Such is reality.

I was offered the opportunity to don the bomb protection gear and take a walk through the school yard to get a feel of what it's like to walk a minefield, albeit a demined one. That remaining 3 percent factor keeps the anxious feeling operative. I was given explicit instructions on how to walk, where to walk, and when to stop forward motion. The demining team was still present and watched me move. Before I started, I looked at the team, thinking that if I sensed their comfort level, I could assume the same level. They were talking amongst themselves, coolly gesturing to make a point and generally conversing in a calm manner. They knew what I was doing but seemed confident that where I was going, they had done their job well. So in I went. As I walked down the specific path I was given, a path I was determined not to get off from, I noticed several spots where special activities had taken place. On one spot a small hole existed, indicating that a mine had been removed. On another spot, small pieces of shrapnel remained in the depression in the ground. At one spot a distance away from my path there remained small mortar shell yet to be disposed of. So there was work yet to done. This being a school ground the 3 percent factor is a factor hard to get by. In reality, though, the 3 percent represents an expression that no matter how thorough an effort to clear the area is, one can never be sure. My having walked the path tells you that I understood the risk and the process.

6

I pulled a picture of Pope John Paul II out of the box I had taken at the Sarajevo sports arena. It was April 13, 1997, when Pope John Paul came to Sarajevo. In my memory, he is the only priest to ever be escorted to Mass by helicopter gunships. I and a coworker of mine sat in my apartment atop the hill above Sarajevo and to the south to watch the Pope pass by below on his way to the Grand Hotel, a new hotel just around the hill from us. We had CNNI on to catch the play-by-play too.

We watched the airport ceremony on CNNI. At the same time, we looked out the apartment window to see everything else that was going on. Across the valley that Sarajevo lies in, I could see the hills beyond where the Serbs had had their big guns that they used to pound the hell out of Sarajevo for four years. Helicopter gunships were hovering along the ridge of these hills as the Pope landed and the ceremony unfolded. I've seen these gunships up close.

Pope John Paul II Arriving at
Sarajevo Stadium for Mass

Pope John Paul II Preparing
to say Mass at the Stadium

They would fly over my apartment almost daily. They would fly low enough that I could almost see the pilot. Their obvious firepower was awesome. As I watched them hover, I imagined how easily it would have been for them to tilt a little forward, dropping their noses, and lining their rocket pods up on a target over the hill. Nothing happened, thankfully, but it certainly would have been a mistake to try. Other gunships were hovering farther away at a higher elevation. During the nights prior to the Pope's arrival I heard a prop-driven airplane circling Sarajevo for hours. I can only assume it was watching night activity with its nighttime instruments. It was up again thc night prior to his arrival.

I was at the Kakanj Power Plant south of the city dealing with a generator rotor problem the day prior to this event of the Pope's coming to town. When I came back to the office, my travel route took me over the bridge into Sarajevo from the airport that was being seen on the TV news. As an aside, it's nice to be insignificant at times. I've traveled the bridge many times, and no one has placed explosives under it because of me. I must tell you about those dumb idiots who removed the mines placed for the passing of the Pope. They were carrying the mines they removed from the bridge just like a person would carry suitcases on the way to the airport. My Mine Safety Awareness training emphasized that all mines are dangerous, even those that have been supposedly disarmed. They can kill. What was displayed on TV was the worst—no, the best—expression of what not to do! They were lucky!

The airport was not too far from where I lived. I could look down the hill and see the route that the Pope would take to his hotel. CNNI told us that he had left the airport, but we knew by the sound of the helicopters approaching that he was already on his way. While the hovering gunships maintained their position over Serb territory, two other gunships moved at the same pace as the popemobile, one on each side of the boulevard at a distance of about three hundred meters was my guess. The one on my side passed directly over my apartment and was going slow enough for me to take pictures. I had no doubt the Pope would get to his hotel room without any trouble.

The day following his arrival the Pope was to say Mass in the stadium. We had to make sure we arrived at the stadium by 0730 to be sure that we could get in. At a scheduled time the stadium was to be secured. Took lots of pictures. Maybe some will turn out.

The stadium has concrete seats and walkways. I don't know if you are aware how cold concrete can get particularly when a cold icy wind continues to sweep across the surface, taking away any heat generated by people standing or sitting. That's what happened. The concrete had had its heat sucked out by the previous night and no sun to put it back came in the morning. It was like standing on a block of ice in your bare feet. We hadn't counted on the cold when we arrived at the inner arena area to participate with the Pope. I foolishly wore just regular shoes because I felt the need to dress up a bit. Well, in my case, when my feet get cold, my whole body rebels, telling me to go to a place of warmth.

I did manage to hold out until 1030. The Pope had entered the stadium and had made a pope-mobile tour around the field, acknowledging those of us who had braved the cold. At 1030, the Pope was just starting his climb up the steps to where he would offer Mass. Unfortunately, the cold had taken its toll on us poorly clothed by then so we decided to retreat to the close-by apartment of a coworker to finish out the Pope's visit in the warmth of a TV room. As I watched the end of the Mass and the final activities of the Pope from comfort, I reflected on the fact that he stayed in the cold stadium. I was seventeen years younger than he was and probably in better health. He stayed, and I didn't. That bothered me. As a diversion from my reflection, during the three hours I was still with the Pope, I watched the gunships still hovering, this time with the stadium as their center of attention. There was a high hill behind Sarajevo in Serb-held territory, where the gunships continued to hover. Sometimes they would descend close to the ground only to rise again after, I guess, verifying that the area of concern was clear. One helicopter kept circling the stadium. SFOR—that's short for Stabilizing Force—military personnel were everywhere. Someone would have to be awfully stupid to try something. I didn't see a smile on any one of them.

A final comment on the Pope's visit: I know that wherever the Pope—any pope—goes, the place is never the same after he leaves. I began to look forward to a different relationship with the Serbs as we tried to carry out some reconstruction efforts in their territory. Up till then they were cutting their nose off to spite their politics. We were waiting with millions of dollars for work to be performed in their area. What was needed was an acknowledgement of the Dayton Accords, and the money would start flowing. Maybe the Pope's visit would be the heat needed to thaw the Serbs out.

Oh, I just remembered another happening regarding the Pope. I was home at that time. The Pope was scheduled to attend a World Youth Day in Denver back in 1993. I was going to give one of my grandsons a Miraculous Medal. At the time one of my cousins lived in Denver, and it so happened that she was friends with the person who would assist the Pope during ritual performances by helping him dress, i.e., help him put on his robes, etc. I saw an opportunity of getting the medal blessed by Pope John Paul II.

Knowing of the friend's duties, I asked my cousin if she could get the medal blessed by the Pope. She said, "Send me the medal, and I'll take care of it." She gave the medal to her friend with the instructions. Her friend took the medal to the Pope, who blessed it but also wore it during his entire time while in Denver. He actually thought it was being given to him to keep until the friend clarified the situation. Anyway, my cousin got the medal back and forwarded it to me with the story of what took place. So I forwarded it on to my grandson.

That was pretty much the end of the story until Pope Benedict XVI decided that Pope John Paul the Great was worthy of being given sainthood. This decision raised the question in my mind about the significance, if any, of this on the medal. So I contacted the Blessed John Paul II Shrine in Washington DC for information.

I was told that JPII's canonization would give the medal a second-class relic classification. I looked up the meaning and found the following definition: "Second-class relics are considered so precious that they are rarely entrusted to individuals but are placed in Faith Communities." I was overwhelmed to say the least! What do I do now, or actually, what should my grandson do with the medal? What began as a simple blessing of a Miraculous Medal had now taken on a major significant condition. I did not want to take the medal back from my grandson, so I put it in a display box to be placed in a spot where he had visual access.

Miraculous Medal Worn and Blessed by Pope John Paul II

7

I pulled out three more documents from the box. One was my Saudi Arabian driver's license. The second was my Saudi Arabian Royal Commission port entry permit. And the third was one Saudi riyal note glued to a piece of poster board. Before going to Saudi Arabia, I was a contract administrator at the Washington Public Power Supply System (WPPSS as it was called in my day).

At the supply system we were involved in the construction of five nuclear electrical power generation stations in the state of Washington. Two were being constructed on the west coast of the state at Satsop and the other three in Hanford near the Tri-City area. I was working at unit numbers 1 and 4 at Hanford. The total capacity of the five stations was designed to supply enough electrical power to support the Northwest into the twenty-first century—at least until 2005 anyway. That was the way it was supposed to work, but that's not the way it ended. In the midseventies the antinuclear activists were in full swing. Nuclear power was branded as anathema to mankind because of its potential harm. Being an ex-nuke sailor familiar with the radiation effects on humans and a participant in the construction of state of the art nuclear power generation facilities, it was difficult for me to see the logic of the activists cause for alarm. But as they say, it's the squeaky wheel that gets the grease. The activists were successful in shutting down the whole industry. In retrospect, I find it difficult not to fault the activists for their contribution to the current pollution problems that the environmental activists are now looking for grease to resolve. I have received several solicitations in the mail since from the environmentalists, which I return asking for an acknowledgement of their participation in the demise of the nuclear power industry. To date, I've had no response.

When I was still at the supply system, I had an occasion to visit a coal-fired power plant being built on the Oregon side of the Columbia River not too far from us at Hanford. The frightening part of this plant was how the coal was processed for burning to heat the water to make steam for the turbine. The coal had to be pulverized to the consistency of talcum powder. This condition put the coal into a highly explosive state even in its stored status. Now that was back in the late seventies, and nothing has happened—no explosion has taken place. But the point is this: there was, and is, more potential for a disaster at the coal-fired plant than at the nuclear plant I was helping to build. To make the point further, I felt the incident at Three Mile Island was an excellent demonstration of the safety features employed by the nuclear industry.

There's another part of this story that I'm not sure preceded or followed the antinuclear protests. The federal organization that controlled the distribution of the electrical power for the Northwest decided after the start of the five plants that, upon reexamination of the power needs, there would not be a need for so much power. The result of this determination led to the supply system having to default on its bonding. The work stopped on the plants, except for one unit. That meant that reduction in supply system personnel was inevitable. And that meant that I chose to beat the exodus, ending up in Saudi Arabia and, among other things, getting a driver's license there. Incidentally, my company placed a bid in the late eighties for several small power plants to be built along the Columbia River to keep up with the power demand.

As with a lot of my decisions regarding my life's unfolding, going to Saudi Arabia was not a traumatic event in the sense that I worried over it. I saw an ad in the local newspaper for contract administrators to help in the construction of a new town being built beside the Red Sea, talked to Jean about it, and answered it. I did not want to stay with the supply system because of too much uncertainty. My decision to go opened up another major chapter in Jean's and my lives. I didn't just go to Saudi Arabia; I started us on a world travel event. In a way I went ahead and checked things out, then Jean decided which place she wanted to see. Two years into my time in Arabia, Jean decided to visit and live there for a while. What an experience for her. She found, among a lot of other findings, how it felt to have no identity as an individual outside of mine. She existed because I did.

It's interesting that in applying for my Saudi Arabian driver's license I did not need to demonstrate my driving ability; I just had to give blood. So I got in line to give blood. When your turn came, you laid on a table that was next to a curtain with a hole in it covered by a flap. You must stick you arm through the hole and lay it on a support on the other side. Then someone prepares your arm to give blood. My guess is that it was a female, although I couldn't be sure. We weren't allowed to peek. As I watched the process unfold, I decided that it was something that I didn't want to go through. I motioned to the person in charge of the line and asked if I really had to do this to get my driver's license. He disinterestedly said, "No. It's just something we do." I took the liberty of opting out and proceeded on to get my license.

I think the reason they want the blood stems from all the traffic accidents that occur. On my first trip in from Jeddah to Yanbu, I went by bus. There's not much to see as the road winds its way across the desert. I did notice wrecked cars on either side of the road occasionally. They seemed to be more than an occasion the farther up the road we went. So I started counting the wrecks. From Jeddah to Yanbu the count was almost four hundred. The distance between the two cities is about four hundred kilometers. Ninety-nine percent of the wrecked cars appeared to be involved in head-on collisions. That's an understandable outcome when driving on a road straight as an arrow with nothing to see but sand and sand dunes on either side of the road. It was interesting that the wrecks were just left on the side of the road. We're talking Mercedes-Benzes, BMWs, Audis, Cadillacs, and other like-priced cars. But not Lincolns, because cars manufactured by the Ford Motor Company were not allowed in Saudi Arabia at that time. As an aside, this first trip to Yanbu began my introduction to a different lifestyle, one that was a little more basic regarding life's little amenities.

Up to now my life really had been operating in a controlled environment. I grew up in a good family setting, got educated in a good family setting, did my time in the strictness of a submarine crew member, had and continue to have a good family of my own, and had great jobs. Now I was entering into a new world of experiences. I was entering a part of the world that I knew existed on the globe but really didn't know anything about. My entry into this part of the world was the third most important move of my life, joining the navy and marrying my wife, Jean, being one and two. The navy brought me to Jean.

I think the best way to explain the contrast of what I was about to enter is to tell you about a painting I had an Iraqi artist do for me. Imagine me standing in front of you, the Iraqi painter—actually, it was her brother—with my right hand raised to enhance my painting request. As I talked to the brother, who worked as a translator for my company, I moved my raised arm across my body from left to right. I said, "Please have your sister paint me a scene that shows Iraq yesterday, today, and tomorrow." About three weeks later he brought me the painting. The artist's depiction of my request was there just like I asked, except that she painted Iraq tomorrow, today, and yesterday. The clash of two cultures can be seen right there. And I was entering the other culture via Saudi Arabia. Upon reflection, I am awestruck at the opportunity I took.

Painting by Iraqi Artist

Driving in Saudi is an experience that proves the tenet of defensive driving. What major roads are in Saudi Arabia are generally good ones. Most are four-lane types with proper traffic sign usage. And the driving surfaces are in good repair. The problems come when local drivers use these roads. I learned very quickly not to move into an intersection after a light change without first counting to five. That allowed the intersection to clear of those local drivers who ignore the red light in their direction. It also gives the local driver on the inside lane time to turn in front of you to the right or, conversely, the local driver on the outside lane to turn in front of you to the left. Complicating this condition is the fact that during the waiting period for light changes, local drivers create additional pseudo-lanes, sometimes as many as three more on each side of a four-lane highway. So now you have five cars abreast, two of which may turn in front of you in either direction at the green light. And you can't forget the cars wanting to turn in the same manner from the opposite side of the highway. An additional caution for any foreign driver was that even if you were not at fault in an accident, your presence placed you at a beginning 10 percent responsibility just because you were there. That was in the early eighties. Maybe it's different today.

My other piece of paper coming out of the box was my Royal Commission Coast Guard pass. This pass was necessary for us to have access to the beach on the Red Sea. Not much else can be said about it.

There was one other piece of paper I pulled out of the box along with my Arabian documents. We Americans always manage to bring a little bit of our homeland culture with us wherever we go, especially when we are working on a long-term project. And whenever project life included members of the employee's families, the transplanted culture includes a lot more. The paper I pulled out was the highlighted script for the acting role I had in the play *Plaza Suite* put on by the Desert Players. The Desert Players acting group was quite active at the Yanbu construction project, having produced many stage plays in addition to *Plaza Suite*. Anyway, I was the bellhop. Normally I was part of the stage crew for the other plays. But as I watched each play, though, I said to myself, "Self, you can do that." Eventually, the director, the wife of one of the project managers, saw my brilliant acting ability and gave me this role. The role of the bellhop was a fundamental role for the story development as seen in my first line: "Everything all right, ma'am?"

Actually, playing a part in any play was not consistent with my character. But it was an opportunity to test the character I had and maybe push the envelope a little. So I tried out for the part. I think the director was being nice to me since I was doing the stage work. No matter. The more I think about it, though, giving something new a try is consistent with my character. That's how I got to Saudi Arabia. Except in this case I was going to expose my character to a sole performance. I had no way to mix in with the crowd. Oh, there were other actors on the stage, but in a sense, each of us was on our own. All of the audience's eyes turn to the actor speaking, expecting to be entertained. Those with experience responded with the calmness of mind that lets them play the part. Those of us without experience respond with the anxiety of the mind that hopes we will play the part. In the end, for the beginner, it comes down to saying the first word and going from there with concentration on the problem at hand. After my final performance, I kept checking my mailbox for the notice of a Tony Award, but alas…

One of the benefits of working on the project in Saudi Arabia was the requirement to renew your visa periodically. That meant you had to leave the country and then reenter to perform the renewal process. This process allowed Jean and me to visit a host of countries, the world being the list to choose where to go. Having spent three years on the project, we were able to visit ten countries over that period. As a result, I was able to stick my hand in all the oceans, except the Arctic and the Antarctic. We lay on the beach on the island of Bali, checked out Stonehenge in England, had our picture taken in the Seoul Tower in Seoul Korea, drove across Spain to the Mediterranean Sea and back to Madrid, stayed in the Dusit Thani Hotel in Bangkok, Thailand, and walked the Great Wall in China, just to name a few.

Oh, we also got to visit the coliseum and the Vatican in Rome. We were able to participate in a tour through the center of St. Peter's Basilica. When we got to the center altar area, the tour guide gave an interesting explanation of why the large columns around the altar had a twisted shape. He said that the columns were not measured correctly and thus were initially much taller than the floor-to-ceiling allowed. So the architect had them twisted to reduce their length, resulting in the proper fit. After the laughter from the group settled down, we proceeded on to the *Pietà*.

8

Remember the brother of the Iraqi artist I was talking to about getting a painting done? We became good friends and had many conversations about Iraq as a country under Hussein and what was happening now. One day I said to him, “Harbi, how would you compare Saddam to other dictators such as Hitler or Stalin?” I was thinking as a person who naturally classifies these kinds of people into evil despots. His immediate response was to vehemently correct me in making such a comparison: I could not compare Saddam to such people! He went to say that Hitler and Stalin were leaders of their people. Saddam wouldn’t even come close as a leader. Saddam did not care for Iraqis. They were only tools for his whims. Harbi had been a history professor at Baghdad University in in his earlier years, so his observation, for me, carried some weight. His comment sent me back to the time of my first entry into Iraq from Kuwait. Our company vehicles were meshed into a military convoy heading toward Baghdad.

It took us two days. On the way, and as we were approaching the outskirts of Baghdad but still in the flats of the desert, I witnessed the sad condition of the Iraqi people as I looked into the soiled face of a small girl standing by the road. She was waving to us as we passed by with a smile that covered her face. She had no shoes on. Her dress was dirty. But there she was, welcoming us as though we were bringing her a new toy. We convoyed on to Baghdad, where we stopped at one of Saddam's sixty-eight palaces and stayed on the second-floor veranda for the next few weeks. I never saw so much Italian marble in my life. Like I say, Harbi's anger had some merit with me.

Saddam Hussein's Palace at Baghdad, Iraq

I went on several convoys while I was in Iraq, mostly to the sites where the captured enemy ammunition (CEA) was being stored by our troops in preparation for elimination. I even got to be a driver of one of the vehicles, one of the armored-up Ford Expeditions we brought in from Kuwait at the start of our project. The company I worked for was one of a group of American companies brought to Iraq to take the CEA from the American military and blow it up. Some of it was given to the Iraqi forces working with our troops for their use. I took some pictures of what we were dealing with. Here's one I took out of my storage box. (Talk about WMD!) During the year that I spent on the project, hundreds of tons per day were being eliminated. When I left, I understood that it would take approximately another two years before the project was completed at the same rate. This was my last work activity too. I was sixty-five. I was ready to retire. I had seen enough of the world.

Typical Pile of Ammunition (WMD) Found on Iraqi Desert

The bottom line here is Jean's and my life was and continues to be a fascinating journey.

EPILOGUE

This book started out with a buffalo head nickel. However, as I went from storage box to storage box, it came to me that as I remarked about what I had picked out each time, I was also coming to an understanding of some concerns of mine that had been festering in the back of my mind for years. Having been born in 1938, my life growth passed through a world culture that saw major changes—major changes to America as well. What follows is a summary of what I now see and understand.

First, I will summarize me. I'm not a scientist or a member of academia, just an old guy who's been to a few places in the world. I do have a college degree though. It's in business management with a concentration in organizational behavior. The best educational opportunities came to me, though, as I moved from a small town in Montana to my current place in Connecticut. My education and experience comes primarily from my exposure to the world through offshore work in places as Saudi Arabia, Turkey, Bosnia, Russia, Iraq, Denmark, and interaction with the local people with whom I worked in each country. I worked in all four corners of America as well as the center too. I've learned which end of the shovel to use and what it takes to build a small town on a desert along side the Red Sea. I know how to demine a mine field. I used a slide rule to calculate the molecular volume of any element on the Chart of Nuclides as I prepared to be a reactor operator in the US Navy in my younger days. My iPhone gives me what I want to know from the Internet now. The local people in the countries I visited or worked in taught me what I did not receive from the books of my formal schooling. The Catholic Church gave me the perspective I needed to put all my experiences into proper context. And I spent six years in the US Navy nuclear submarine service. I taught Catholic Christian doctrine for over forty-five years and completed a four-year course in advanced biblical history. Being in my seventy-seventh year of life, I believe I have an understanding of what makes the world go around. One more thing, each time I returned to America, the contrast from where I had been working was overwhelming. This not to blow my own horn but to lay the foundation of how I see what is in front of me now. And for the rest of you for that matter.

I'm an observer now, so I can say whatever I want. Being an observer means, among other things, that no one is vying for my attention because I need very little of what is on the market. No sense wasting money or time on the likes of me.

(By the way, I'm not complaining. Just an observation.) As I look around, extending my vision to the ends of the living world, it appears to me that there are certain trends of human conduct today that follow old paths, paths that remind me of the admonishment, "Those who fail to learn from the past are doomed to repeat it." At the same time, there are new habits being formed by the young that don't even consider the past. Don't misunderstand me now; there are a large number of people who are going about their lives comfortable and happy. Unfortunately, though, they will be affected by what's going on too.

If we take a rudimentary look back in time at the rise and fall of each culture, I think we can see a common pattern. Until the Hebrews came to be, in cultures such as the Egyptians, the Romans, the Greeks, the Bedouins, the Assyrians, the North and South American inhabitants, etc., we see that each was based on a humanistic view of the local world around each. That view relied on a ruling structure contained in one element of the culture that came from dominant power supported by fear of reprisal and/or a convincing "religion" that justified leadership entitlement. As time went on, however, those in power became complacent, expecting their position to be permanent but finding that those in the lower classes or other cultures did not agree. Hence the rise and fall of cultures over time.

Okay, now the American situation. As you look around the public square in America these days and see what is being said, written, visualized, etc., the observation can be made that the country appears to have reached a plateau of human achievement. The iPhone pretty much describes the status of things. It's the result of President Kennedy's instruction to go to the moon. His instruction took us from the vacuum tube to the microchip. It also reflects the history of America's development since 1776, which allowed Kennedy to give such an instruction.

However, as I said, we've reached a plateau, a plateau that is akin to other plateaus reached by previous dominant cultures. The Roman Empire comes to mind. The Ottoman Empire comes to mind. Various European cultures come to mind. Then there's the Communist Empire. Each reached a plateau by an emperor/king/dictator dominating power structure. Except America. America achieved its plateau through individual effort put forth within a family structure operating in a community of families with a strong religious base and a government of the people.

Unfortunately, today, that support base has changed, and America is now resting on its laurels. Parallel to going to the moon, academia began to adapt a liberal attitude with the "free speech movement" in the 1960s along with the "sexual revolution," which continues today. At the same time, American exceptionalism is being challenged as an expression of the American can-do spirit. In a sense, instead, it's "eat, drink, and be merry" time.

If we don't pay attention, we will begin to lose the sense of how we got here. We are already seeing a deterioration of self-reliance. Our federal and state governments are wanting increased control of what a person can do or not do. *Income inequality*, *fair wage*, "You didn't build that," "Take that cross down," *common core*, and "Contraception is a woman's health issue" are becoming the standard phrases of the public square.

The question now becomes "Where do we go from here?" Well, there is another plateau above the human one. No culture to date has risen to its level. This level rests in the metaphysical world where a person can see the ultimate outcome of mankind's eschatological state. The American culture has the best chance of moving upward. But only if the people recall what the elements of the previous struggle are that were developed by the family and religious base. Finally, we need to analyze St. John Paul II's concepts of "original man" and "historical man" to give us the full picture.

Let's review the American culture. It starts at the Declaration of Independence and follows through with the Constitution.

The Declaration of Independence Preamble

> When in the Course of human events it becomes necessary for one people to dissolve the political bands which have connected them with another and to assume among the powers of the earth, the separate and equal station to which the Laws of Nature and

> of Nature's God entitle them, a decent respect to the opinions of mankind requires that they should declare the causes which impel them to the separation.
>
> We hold these truths to be self-evident, that all men are created equal, that they are endowed by their Creator with certain unalienable Rights, that among these are Life, Liberty and the pursuit of Happiness.—That to secure these rights, Governments are instituted among Men, deriving their just powers from the consent of the governed,—That whenever any Form of Government becomes destructive of these ends, it is the Right of the People to alter or to abolish it, and to institute new Government, laying its foundation on such principles and organizing its powers in such form, as to them shall seem most likely to effect their Safety and Happiness.

From this base, those people having come together from primarily Great Britain, though some came from France and maybe some from Spain and Italy, decided on a new form of government. Thus, we have a constitution that begins as follows.

Preamble of the United States Constitution

> We the People of the United States, in Order to form a more perfect Union, establish Justice, insure domestic Tranquility, provide for the common defence, promote the general Welfare, and secure the

> Blessings of Liberty to ourselves and our Posterity, do ordain and establish this Constitution for the United States of America.

And so began another attempt by human persons to develop a way of living together in common purpose, except this time without the historical concept of special entitlement because of family, position, religious right, or any other reason that made a group of human persons consider themselves unique in the world. This time, the rule of law would prevail. What began almost four hundred years ago with the landing at Plymouth Rock continues today. However, historical stresses are reappearing that are placing a challenge before the people, stresses that could bring down even the great American experiment if not dealt with.

First, before we get into the actions of human persons, we have to discover what makes a human person. Notice I am not making reference to a human being. There is a significant difference. Simply put, the descriptor *human being* merely identifies an animal that walks upright on two legs. Changing *being* to *person* adds the metaphysical dimension to this animal that can now look into a mirror and state emphatically that it knows what it sees. This additional dimension was given to the human being by the Creator, who is "First Cause of all." This gift was given at the moment human procreation took place, i.e., conception. No other animal benefited from such a participation. No other animal enjoys free will, which was another part of the gift. If there were, the movie *Planet of the Apes* would be a true depiction of another life-form. So being unique in the universe puts a special responsibility on human persons. We are above the level of the survival of the fittest. We must, then, see to the survival of all life-forms within the context of nature's evolution.

All that being said, humans, since time began, had come together to try to live together in harmony. It is human nature to want the simple things of life. Look at most of the people around the world. I can point to Russians, Bosnians, Turks, Saudi Arabians, Danes, Serbs, Croatians, and Americans in the places where I've worked and other nationalities whose countries I've only visited. They want to live a life of comfort, joy, achievement, happiness—all ways that do away with fear, want, domination, and all things negative. It is the nature of man. Our image includes the desire of homogeneous living. It is our nature to say hi to a passing stranger or "Can I help you with that?" It is when, as George Orwell said in his book A*nimal Farm*, "some people are more equal than others" where the problem of power comes into play. On the other hand, it is also a part of the nature of man that in the mix of persons, some are leaders and some are followers, neither of which is more important than the other. Coupled with these characteristics is the tendency of a group to want to establish order such that each member can do what it wants to do or has agreed to do for the group. However, all human persons recognize that the environment/culture in which they currently live is the one they have to abide by. The professor in my college social science (an oxymoron if I ever heard of one) class remarked that even mentally disturbed persons seek to control their lives.

The most fundamental arrangement of human persons is the family—the traditional concept, not the bastardization that is currently being promoted pretty much around the Western world. A family consists of a man, a woman, and a child or children. Go back in history as far as you want to go and check out what a family consists of, and you will find support for my definition. Go to any culture in the world. Select any period of that culture, and you will see the existence of the traditional family structure. Oh, I'm sure you will find the nontraditional one—a small element, as an exception to the rule—but there is always 10 percent who "don't get the word." I will, on the other hand, give the 10 percent a quality of making sure the other 90 keep on their toes, until now.

I have to bring in another element into this discussion before I go any further. This element will help round out the scope of living life.

There is this intellect that I know about. It's been a thorn in my side ever since I could make decisions on my own. What follows is a short discussion on it.

The devil. Who in the hell is he—or she? I'll stick with "he" for this effort, even though there is no gender. Why do I care who or what he is anyway? If he impacts my life, I would care. So does he? Let's see.

I only know of his existence because I was told about him. Until I learned of him, I viewed all the external influences on me as interactions with my five senses. (The same goes for my guardian angel by the way.) I would take the sensory input and draw whatever conclusion I might have through my cognitive activity to determine what I was to do next. No problem. But now I know about him.

Actually, if I'd read ancient history to a much greater depth, I might have concluded that perhaps there were some "others" simply because of the natural human condition to assign the unknown to another intelligence outside the body and hidden in the "out there." Just look at the totems, the monoliths, and the stories about the sun god or the river god or the myriad of other gods used to explain what man currently didn't understand but to which he had to put a name or a story. These explanations continued even when the story was told by Moses back in the days of Egyptian domination of Northern Africa and the slavery of a certain group of people, referred to as the Hebrews, under Pharaoh.

The Hebrews taught that a supreme being existed that was not a product of human imagination but who, in fact, created us humans in his image and likeness. Moses, one of the Hebrews, wrote stories telling how this supreme being created everything. These stories, called the Torah, were written six or seven thousand years ago and have become the first five books of the Christian Bible. It turns out Jesus Christ, born just over two thousand years ago, provided valid proof, through his teaching, his death, and resurrection, that Moses wrote it right.

One of the things Moses wrote about was the existence of spiritual intellects called angels. These intellects were given a decision to make just after their creation as to whether they wanted to remain with God or not. Some did, some didn't. Those that didn't immediately saw what they had given up but also found that the decision they made was a permanent one. Being complete at creation meant learning about life, so to speak, was unnecessary. They had all they needed to make an unmitigated freewill decision. It seems pride had driven them to this end. They concluded that they should be able to enjoy the entitlements apparent to them in their being. Except that God did not create them equal to himself. Unfortunately, their pride then drove them further to vengeance—vengeance against this Creator. But they had no retributive act possibilities against God because, well, because he was the Creator God. As I mentioned, God created humans also. In their (being a triune God, Father, Son, and Holy Spirit) image and likeness they made humans. What that meant was that in the image part, humans had basic characteristics that God had. In the likeness part, though, humans had to develop, through a life progression, the remaining part that, upon completion of an earthly period, the human would have come to the existence intended by God in an eternal state in relationship to God. As with the angels, humans had free will. But in variance with the angels, humans were given a period of performance in which to use their free will to respond to God's will, as He determined, for each of them on their road to eternal happiness—or the other.

The beauty of free will and at the same time the potential negative eternal consequence of it rests in the no decision. Being able to say no makes the yes absolutely personal and a reflection of the human's ultimate desire. Unfortunately, saying yes to a detrimental option can be quite akin to some of the angelic outcomes.

Further, as implied above, we humans are not alone as we progress. There are four intellectual elements to every decision we humans make. They are human, God (composed of the Trinity of persons), good angels, and bad angels. The process begins with the human. Something comes to mind that requires a decision. Let's categorize it as a want. The stimulation of this want can come from an internal or external source keeping in mind that there is a continuous interaction between the two. It is a combination of nature and nurture. Regardless, there must be reaction to it by the human, consciously or subconsciously. Let's start with God's input.

To make use of the capabilities after the fall as God intended, a list of Ten Commandments were posted to which the humans must adhere to achieve His intended result. The ten were grouped into two categories, one to know the required relationship to establish with God and the other to establish a relationship with another human or group of humans.

When God created the human, he gave him certain characteristics, e.g., awareness of self, free will, cognitive ability, associative capability with other humans, and reproductive ability just to name a few. (Use of the male gender descriptor in this writing includes both male and female references consistent with Moses's explanation in his first book, Genesis.) With these characteristics, humans could conduct their lives as they saw fit. The outcome of decisions over time gives the human knowledge of its status with God and its fellow humans.

The bad angel, described variously as the devil, Beelzebub, Lucifer, and the evil one, having made the prideful decision to reject God's offering, cannot act directly against God to extract his revenge. Being an intellectual spirit, however, still gave him other options. If he couldn't act directly against God, he could act against God's creative outcomes and potential outcomes. If he could interfere with the creative process, he could conclude that revenge had been achieved. But that which was being created had to know what revenge meant, otherwise, it would be like smashing a rock into pieces. All you end up with is smaller rocks. Therefore the only creation of God's that can see and feel the act of revenge is a human.

There are two acts of creation that God performed that the devil could act upon for his revenge. The first was when humans were still in the garden of Eden. This is the place where God put the first humans, Adam and Eve, to live a life that included a face-to-face relationship with Him under specific conditions: "Don't eat the apple!" The second creative act is the one that God participates in with humans, that of their procreative effort. There is a third act of the devil that affects those humans already pursuing their life's work, which can be seen as interfering in the end of the creative act of God. An interference in a human's development in achieving the likeness of God, if you will.

It was when Adam and Eve did eat the apple that a second class of angels came into the picture. In the garden, humans didn't need any other intellect with whom to interact other than God. Unless, of course, if God decided to make some changes, but he didn't. The good angels and the bad angels were around, but their function relative to humans were not yet defined. So, after the dinner and the expulsion from the garden, the good angels took on a new task. Their assignment can be summed up in the following prayer.

> Angel of God, my guardian dear, to whom God's love commits me here. Ever this day be at my side to light, to guard, to rule and guide. Amen.

Now, before I go on, I must address the significance of the eating of the apple. As Moses described the apple tree, he called it the tree of the knowledge of good and evil. So we can conclude that it is knowledge that Adam and Eve didn't need or know about in the garden. But when they did eat and became aware of this knowledge, the whole of humanity had to operate under a new set of rules. Why did such a dramatic and far-reaching effect on the relationship between Adam and Eve, and thus humanity, and God take place? Why did God take such an action? It was a simple act on the part of Adam and Eve, was it not? Why not just an admonition to not do it again?

We need to look at the tree again. It is a living thing that has food in the form of fruit hanging from its branches. The food is apparently special in that it can open up a human's current view of his world. I think, though, we are dealing with a metaphor for self-control. It also implies that sufficient are the other trees, i.e., those that describe the relationship God intended for the humans in the garden. However, in order for a human to exercise its free will in this relationship, limits had to be put in place. Remember the value of the no decision.

The apple has a delicious taste. What does that mean in terms of knowledge of good and evil? For someone, this knowledge has value. Was this knowledge a prerogative of God alone? Why was it important for humans not to know the difference? Without that knowledge, all acts of the human would be consistent with God's intentions. Did it bring into human conduct the act of judgment on actions taken, judgment being a prerogative of God alone? To take such a dramatic and consequential action—what the tree had to signify by the eating of the apple—put humans into God's realm of existence before humans were ready as defined by God.

What better way then for the bad angel to achieve its revenge than to convince the human to decide to violate God's plan by choosing to acquire knowledge that maybe he wasn't ready for because of the idea that man's likeness to God had not yet come to fruition as intended by God. The human has free will, right? And so he did. The human made the decision, but the bad angel got to put the "mark on the wall."

Now we come to the next opportunity for revenge. This one has been relatively easy for the bad angel to work through. As it turns out, there is no more explosive and pleasurable emotional release for the human than the sexual climax. Once experienced, forever desired. And an excellent opportunity for manipulation too. In the original context of the sexual intimacy, God instructed humans to leave their parents and come together as man and wife and to become as one. The instructions were not broad but specific. Sexual intercourse was to be only between a man and a woman bound to each other for life.

Sexual intimacy comprises two basic outcomes: procreation and expression of love. Thus, the act should only be carried out as above. The problem is, though, as also stated above, the act is such a pleasurable experience. It is said to have resulted in the generation of the oldest profession. What an opportunity for the bad angel! He has been able to convince the humans that pleasure was prime and anybody can do it. It doesn't really matter if the two are married, in love, or just out for a good time. So, again, revenge is marked on the wall.

In this case, his wall gets marked on in the millions per day. I'm surprised he has enough pencils! Keep in mind that the humans are making the choices, not him. He's just painting a submissive picture.

Finally, there is an end time for each human. As God set it up, humans each can finish their time on earth as He determines. Free will, though, can accept it or change it as the human chooses within God's chosen limits. The bad angel has another opportunity to interfere with God's plan, convincing the human to avoid all the pain and suffering and end it all now. Another mark on the wall!

Let's now talk about the good angel. These angels are at the beck and call of God. One of their tasks is to interact with humans as needed to give guidance that supports God's plan for that human. Just as with God and the bad angel, we are not talking about having a face-to-face conversation but through indirect mind stimulation or other attention getting techniques. There have been face-to-face conversations in the past where an angel communicated directly as directed by God. The Annunciation where Mary was given the option of participating with the Holy Spirit to conceive and bring into the world Jesus Christ is one example. There have been more, but I want to dwell on the guardian angel.

A guardian angel's task was to attend to a specific human through its life period that John Paul the Great, in his lectures on "The Theology of the Body," called the historical man period. Obviously, it was a natural to call the garden period the original man period. The period after the historical man, again, naturally, was named the eschatological man period. But I digress. The good angel is concerned with the human from birth to death, doing whatever it can to steer the human in the right direction toward God, trying to counter the human's bad choices and the bad angel's influence. Keep in mind that God, as Jesus taught, was always in the lead trying to show the path to Him that each human should take. Further, the human need not fear the bad angel or his own stupidity. He need only put his faith in God. Easier said than done.

Okay, we now have all the players on the field. The human person is the quarterback, God is the head coach, the devil and his henchmen are the opposing team, the guardian angel is the sum of sideline support, and the offensive team is the rest of humanity. We can now go back to Plymouth Rock and set the stage for the American experience.

For the first time in recorded history, at least that which I have read, the opportunity presented itself for human persons to set the stage for a heart-to-heart talk on how they can live together without some special human power telling them what the rules are. Plymouth Rock was kind of a stepping stone for persons fed up with kings and queens and other entitled persons. They all could speak their minds without reprisal. And so they did. Their actions spoke as loud as their words. Beginning with their understanding of the human person that "they are endowed by their Creator with certain unalienable Rights, that among these are Life, Liberty and the pursuit of Happiness," they continued to declare that as humans, they could establish a government that saw almost no inequality among themselves, thus they wrote, "We the People of the United States, in Order to form a more perfect Union, establish Justice, insure domestic Tranquility, provide for the common defence, promote the general Welfare, and secure the Blessings of Liberty to ourselves and our Posterity, do ordain and establish this Constitution for the United States of America." I say almost; however, while the Constitution did not discriminate, there were still personal biases present in the people who came together to write. Not all of these biases could be cast aside at the time of writing either. In Article IV, Section 2, Clause 3, it was written "No Person held to Service or Labour in one State, under the Laws thereof, escaping into another, shall, in Consequence of any Law or Regulation therein, be discharged from such Service or Labour, but shall be delivered up on Claim of the Party to whom such Service or Labour may be due." Thus, one of the biggest problems that existed and, in fact, could not be solved at the time of writing the Constitution, was slavery. Within the minds of the writers the words *service or labour* could be defined as needed, thus slavery remained an issue. To try to deal with such personal biases, brought with them from their past, would have defeated the whole effort. The problem was left to future dialogue. And it was a wise move because establishing a new form of government was paramount. The framers had included a method to amend the Constitution so that when agreeable minds came together, changes could be made in a rational and reasonable way. Slavery was addressed in the Thirteenth Amendment. Incidentally, in 226 years, only twenty-seven amendments have been ratified, which says a lot for the original document.

But now we have a problem. In those 226 years America has become a superpower through the individual and collective efforts of its citizens. Americans can take any question or problem and arrive at a solution that benefits themselves and, in fact, the world. I've heard it said regarding Americans that "thought is action." When I was at a meeting in Russia to carry out a task that needed Russian approval, we Americans came to the meeting with the solution but had to go through an hour-and-a-half discourse by the Russians before our solution was approved. In other places in the world where Americans were doing work for the local government, we were always seen as the "people who could get things done!"

Our schools were second to none. Our factories were efficient with improvements in the process always taking place. You name it, we could produce it. Families were the center of every community. That is, until Americans began to think they had it made, akin to the way the Romans, etc., did. But now, we face challenges, albeit different from the Romans, etc., in culture. The similarity of human expectations of self-entitlement is there also. And so began a confrontational period in the twentieth century, fed by memories of the previous centuries, that bring us Americans to the brink of European failures akin to the kings, queens, religious, pharaohs, and dictators of the past. I can best sum it up as follows.

We see ourselves as human beings rather than as human persons. As I said before, a person can look into a mirror and understand and know what it sees. A being lives under the premise of survival of the fittest. This attitude makes it easy to accept the killing of over fifty million lives before each has the opportunity to develop as it is capable of doing. It allows us to disregard the family structure. It allows us to disregard God. It allows us to redefine God in terms of the state as god. Under Communism in Russia, the children were taught that the state was indeed god, and therefore the state would provide what is needed. We are going back to the humanistic view of reality of the past. We have decided that the Constitution is a living document whose words are adjustable to current moods and practices. Amendments take too long.

What used to be family responsibilities in this country are now becoming state entitlements. Some parents—or should I say nonparents—let the community raise their children rather than set the rules at home based on moral, ethical, and religious principles that have been the basis of this country since its beginning. Unfortunately though, today's standards of conduct do not always find their basis in these time-honored principles.

On the other hand, maybe we are going through another adjustment period initiated by a higher authority as has happened in the past, designed to bring humanity up another level beyond the totem pole. But until we recall who is the coach and who is the quarterback, we will suffer the repeat of the past.

A FINAL THOUGHT

I must tell about an experience I just had while visiting my son and his family out west and up north in Washington State concerning a wineglass full of wet sand. My son lives in what can be described as a liberal enclave of high-tech people. I'm not one of them. I'm told I used to be one of them. But I did some traveling around the world and the United States and got myself educated in reality. I shouldn't be too hard on them, I guess. They're educated also. This insolated use of an education is an issue, I'm afraid, that I need to defer until another page.

I had come to the West Coast visit with my brother, who had had a defibrillator installed in his chest a couple weeks prior. My younger brother who lives in Montana and I decided we should see for ourselves where our older brother stood. You see, we lie to each other when it comes to health things. And we always inform each other of things already done, not to be done. Anyway, my brother looked good, and we decided he was in good hands with Andi, his wife. So I was back with my son and his family. He decided to take me to their favorite Mexican restaurant. My son had been there often enough that he and the owner were on friendly terms. He introduced me before we were seated in a booth along the left wall. There was another set of booths on the opposite wall. They were all filled with families and a lot of talking. Three booths down on the opposite wall a man and his girlfriend were just finishing up and were engaged in conversation. I noticed that he gave me a nod as I looked his way. I returned the acknowledgment. Shortly after that he and his friend rose from their booth and passed by our booth on the way out. I paid no more mind and continued talking with my son and his fiancée. Not more than three minutes later he turned to our table. He had a plastic freezer-type bag in his hand.

He apologized for interrupting our dinner, but he said he would only take a moment. He began to tell me that he had been waiting in the booth in the back corner for his friend to arrive, but he didn't show. He had something to give him. As he was talking he had the freezer bag hung loosely in both hands. He continued to talk as I scanned the bag wondering why it had a wineglass filled with what appeared to be damp sand. He said that he thought I would be the only one around who would understand what he had in the bag and what he was about to tell me. He went on that he had been to France just recently and had taken a special trip to the beach at

Normandy. The sand in the wineglass was from that beach. Since his friend did not show up, he offered it to me.

You can imagine the number of thoughts that went through my head in a very short time. What's really in the bag? Who is this guy? What's he selling? What's the wineglass for? Why me? As he was talking, I scanned the bag closely. It was indeed sand. But what kind of sand? It was damp. Why was it damp? It was damp, he said, because he wanted to preserve the sand as it was on the beach. Sounded logical. Okay, what's he selling? Nothing. His comments did not imply wanting anything for the sand. Nothing explicit either. What's the wineglass for? I thought, *How better to express the essence of the sand that supported American military boots racing from the landing crafts to the safety of the distant grassy areas away from the water. How better to contain and memorialize the blood of the Americans who tried to fight their way inland but didn't make it. A fine wine it is!*

Why me? Well, it was my baseball cap and my age. My cap has a set of submarine dolphins sewn on the front with my boat's name and number on top and below the set. That told him that I was ex-military. My age told him that I would remember the sixth of June 1944. Wearing my hat at my age told him that I would hold such memories in high regard. It was a no-brainer there.

Who was this guy? I could only speculate. He didn't spend a long time at our table. He just wanted to pass the sand of Normandy on to someone who understood. That only took about three minutes. But for him to take the time to scoop the sand into a wineglass tells me that his friend, who didn't show up, must have had a direct connection to the beach either himself or through his father. In any event, the act was one of great personal significance. Nothing told me that this guy was a sham or a wise guy looking to make a fool of an old salt. I took him at his word.

Perhaps I accepted the guy's story because of other meetings with strangers who came to me because of my cap. I was standing in the security line at the Long Beach Airport waiting for my turn at the detectors a few months ago. A man passing by the line stopped up short after seeing my cap. He walked over and said, "I was on that boat. I was part of the last crew before its decommissioning." I was dumbfounded! I said, "I was part of the commissioning crew." The boat went into service in the early sixties and out of service in the mideighties. Then another time I was coming out of Mass one Saturday evening when another man was walking past on his way to his car. He too stopped short when he saw my cap. He called out, "I was on that boat in the seventies." We talked for a moment about our times on the boat, and then he went on. How far can you extend coincidence?

Let's see how far. In early November of the same year, I was reading an article in the local newspaper about a nun who had previously been a nurse from Massachusetts in her younger days. She had joined the Army Nurse Corps in 1943 where she became part of the medical group that followed the soldiers landing on the beaches at Normandy on June 6, 1944. Her medical group walked the sands after coming ashore off an LST on June 17, 1944 to begin providing the massive medical help needed as the invasion proceeded inland. Reading further, I realized that her convent was just up the road from where I was living. As I read on, it became clear to me that the sand I had really belonged to her. After all, her footprints were probably mixed into the particles of sand in the wineglass. And who better to contemplate what else was in the sand? Her first twenty-eight days in Normandy, the article reports, were spent participating in the treatment of five thousand wounded soldiers, which included 2,600 operations. So I decided to take the wineglass of sand to her at the abbey. I began the process by writing a letter to her at the Benedictine Abbey of Regina Laudis, located in Bethlehem, Connecticut. After a couple weeks, I received a letter back from Mother Irene telling me that she would be delighted to have the Normandy Beach sand.

We had just finished enduring a nor'easter the day previous to our travels. There was a lot of snow with a hard crust on top. As a kid in Washington State, I would slide down the hill on my stomach in this kind of snow. What fun. Anyway, I had asked my parish priest to accompany me because we were going to a place where a group of nuns seeking to maintain 350 acres of farm and woodland lived "according to the principles of traditional Benedictine stewardship and contemporary ecological awareness" as their booklet describing their *Women in Chant* CD states. (I love chant, so I had to buy their CD on my way out after the visit.) I also needed Father because I wanted someone who would be more sensitive to the respect and deference to be given to such a group and thus would keep me in line. I was already filled with nervous anticipation of meeting Mother Irene, so I needed grounding. Father was also a native of the area, spending his many years in the priesthood in a few of the local parishes. So he had the history. It had been around fifteen years since his last visit, though. But that was all right. His memory was good.

During the trip up to the abbey, we didn't get a chance to talk about the abbey buildings. So my mind's eye was still looking for a relatively large brick structure facing the entrance of the acreage and a lot of statues and flower gardens aesthetically placed along the approach to the building. As I drove up the road, I was looking for the match to my prefabricated vision. There was snow on the ground, so I didn't expect to see the flower gardens, but at least the statues would be there. Well we finally turned into this nondescript driveway just able to let one vehicle pass through the gate. The driveway led up toward some buildings that upon closer look did show possibilities for some group living there. Seeing a couple of cows in the field off to the left, I was reminded of a typical farm layout, which of course it was. There was one building at the end of the driveway that seemed to have an entryway similar to a reception area to an office perhaps.

With Father's prompt, we took a chance and went through the first door, then through some vertically hung and overlapping wide clear plastic strips to gain entrance to the final door that brought us indeed into a reception area. These plastic strips did a fine job of keeping the heat in and the cold out. The foyer was "decorated" in unfinished wooden one-by-eights and tens going floor to ceiling with two doors, one at each side of the near back wall. Neither door had knobs or handles to allow opening from this area. One door had a slot for notes and letters to be dropped in. This door also had a wooden grating that allowed the person on the other side to talk to people on our side. I could see a couple of phones hanging on the wall. Before we entered the final door, Father had pushed the buzzer to alert the appropriate person inside that visitors had arrived. As it happened, and probably a lot, Father reached out of the door and pushed the buzzer a second time a few minutes later. A couple minutes after that, a nun appeared at the other side of the grated door, greeting us and asking if I was the one who was to meet with Mother Irene. I nodded. She went on to say that another nun would be along to take us to the tower where Mother Irene would be. The phone rang just then, which she answered, and then she disappeared from where she came. Our escort appeared shortly, and we proceeded to the tower.

The sister on reception duty said that normally Mother Irene would walk down to the reception area and meet her visitors there, but because of the ice and snow, Mother Irene thought it best to have us come up the hill to the tower. We followed the sister outside, expecting to walk a short distance up the hill, but she said we would need to drive. We could follow her truck up there. My mind's eye was quickly getting a new vision of the abbey. My mind's eye had to change its attitude about time and schedule too. Father did mention that the abbey would not necessarily be on the same schedule as we on the outside would be. He also said that time would have a different character. I was learning fast that my time frame was not their time frame. But then again, why should it? Theirs obviously does not look outward but inward to their own needs as they would go through their routine of life. I'm just a momentary intrusion here. At the same time, Mother Irene did not consider me an intrusion. She listened to my sand story again even though I had written the same thing in my letter.

As we drove up to the tower, which actually appears to be several separate living quarters at various points along the road, we passed by some rather large trucks that the nuns apparently use in their farming activities. We stopped in front the quarters where Mother Irene was staying. I was told to park my vehicle farther away from the path of the oncoming trucks that can come from the rise above than I was doing. I complied readily. We were escorted to the quarters that had at least two floors. Inside, while waiting for Mother Irene to appear, I noticed the room had fewer amenities than I had in the tent I lived in when I was in Iraq. The walls were not painted except for maybe some preservative to maintain the natural state of the wood. I don't know. There was a wall of books beside the door from where Mother Irene eventually entered. There was a large window that allowed one to see over the stairs going to the second floor, the trees, and open fields descending slowly away toward the road below.

She was small of stature but had a strong presence. She immediately arranged for us all to sit at her table. She moved a little slowly but not bad for someone eight-seven years old. Another sister who helped arrange the meeting attended to our initial meeting amenities and then excused herself to see to her waiting duties. Shortly after she went outside, we saw her through the window as she and a man began hoisting a Christmas tree up to the second floor above us. They couldn't move it up the stairway because it was too wide at the base. They walked up the steps, carrying the tree up by reaching over the railing and manhandling it up with outstretched arms.

The table was a plain one, similar to the one I have in my basement, except mine had a smoother finish. The chairs were a straight-back type where the outside wood strip beginning at the seat made a rising rounded frame to the other side of the seat, holding the rounds appropriately in place. Mother Irene began the conversation with a motion to the wineglass of sand I had yet to put on the table. I mumbled something along the line that it seemed like she should have the sand because she had been there. Then I proceeded to relate the story of how the sand came to me and quickly brought my comments to a close because it didn't make sense to tell her what she already knew. I turned to a piece of paper I had brought with me. My grandson Matthew, an avid WWII buff at ten years of age, had his mother send me a question that had been on his mind about Normandy. I copied it down from the e-mail so that I would get it right when I asked the question for him. He asked, "Was it as dark and cloudy as I have seen in books and on TV on D-day?" Instead of reading it to her, I just gave the paper to her to read. Mother Irene's answer was simply yes. I saw in her face that she was looking back to those days as she answered. For a moment she was not with us.

One question I had asked Father on the way up to the abbey was how we would know when it was time to leave. He replied that she would let us know. And she did. It was not a statement on the issue but a switching the conversation from me to him. We both knew it was time to leave and quickly brought the meeting to a close. We had spent over a half hour with her, so it was time. I asked to have a picture taken with her, a request she accommodated after showing a wry smirk, as though it was something she could or would endure.